COLLEGE CHINESE

Revised Edition, Volume Two

COLLEGE CHINESE
Revised Edition, Volume Two

a first-year textbook

Shou-ying Lin

Cheng & Tsui Company

First published by the Council on East Asian Studies,
Harvard University

Cheng & Tsui Company
25 West Street
Boston, Massachusetts 02111-1268 USA

Library of Congress Catalogue Number: 93-072860

Set of four-volume paperback books: ISBN: 0-88727-188-X

Audio-cassette tapes are also available from Publisher

Calligraphy by Diana Wang
Cover design by Kenje Ogata

Cover calligraphy taken from rubbings of running characters
by the famous Jin dynasty calligrapher Wang Xizhi (321-379).

Printed in the United States of America

College Chinese
Revised Edition, Volume Two

Contents

Traditional Characters

LESSON I

New Words (traditional characters)

1.	學生	n	xuésheng	student
2.	老師	n	lǎoshī	teacher
3.	您	p	nín	you (polite form)
4.	是	v	shì	to be
5.	美國	n	Měiguó	U.S.A.
6.	人	n	rén	person
7.	嗎	par	ma	question particle
8.	我	p	wǒ	I, me
9.	不	adv	bù	not, no
10.	中國	n	Zhōngguó	China
11.	你	p	nǐ	you
12.	這	sp	zhè, zhèi	this
13.	書	n	shū	book
14.	那	sp	nà, nèi	that
15.	報	n	bào	newspaper
16.	他	p	tā	he

I

學生	老師，您是美國人嗎？
老師	我不是美國人，我是中國人。你是美國人嗎？
學生	我是美國人。

II

學生	這是中國書嗎？
老師	這是中國書。
學生	那是中國書嗎？
老師	那不是中國書，那是中國報。

III

老師	他是學生嗎？
學生	他是學生。
老師	他是中國學生嗎？
學生	他不是中國學生，他是美國學生。

LESSON II

New Words (traditional characters)

1.	有	v	yǒu		to have
2.	一	nu	yī		one
3.	張	m	zhāng		measure word
4.	紙	n	zhǐ	（張）*	paper
5.	兩	nu	liǎng		two
6.	很	adv	hěn		very
7.	大	adj	dà		big
8.	小	adj	xiǎo		small
9.	沒有	v	méiyou		to have not, to be without
10.	本	m	běn		measure word
11.	舊	adj	jiù		old *things*
12.	新	adj	xīn		new
13.	好	adj	hǎo		good
14.	多	adj	duō		many
15.	老	adj	lǎo		old *people*
16.	少	adj	shǎo		few
17.	三	nu	sān		three
18.	個	m	gè		measure word *people*
19.	北京	n	Běijīng		Beijing (Peking)

---

*Words in parentheses in this column are the measure words most often associated with the preceding nouns

- 3 -

I

學生1	我有一張紙。你有紙嗎?
學生2	我有紙。我有兩張紙。
學生1	那兩張紙大嗎?
學生2	這兩張紙不大,這兩張紙很小。
學生1	你有中國報嗎?
學生2	我沒有中國報。

II

學生1	這兩本書是舊書嗎?
學生2	那兩本書不是舊書,是新書。
學生1	新書好嗎?
學生2	新書不好,舊書好。很多舊書很好。
學生1	這兩本新書很大。
學生2	那兩本新書不大,這本舊書大。

III

老師1	新學生多嗎?
老師2	新學生不多。老學生多,新學生少。
老師1	那三個新學生是北京人嗎?
老師2	不是北京人。很少學生是北京人。

New Words (traditional characters)

1.	毛筆	n	máobǐ	（枝）	writing brush
2.	鋼筆	n	gāngbǐ	（枝）	fountain pen
3.	枝	m	zhī		measure word
4.	的	par	de		subordinating particle
5.	鉛筆	n	qiānbǐ	（枝）	pencil
6.	長	adj	cháng		long
7.	短	adj	duǎn		short
8.	們	suf	-men		plural pronoun suffix
9.	黑板	n	hēibǎn	（個）	blackboard
10.	乾淨	adj	gānjing		clean
11.	本子	n	běnzi	（個，本）	notebook
12.	對不對		duìbuduì		is it right?
13.	對了	v	duìle		(it is) right
14.	朋友	n	péngyou*		friend
15.	英國	n	Yīngguó		England
16.	英文	n	Yīngwén		English language
17.	中文	n	Zhōngwén		Chinese language

---

*Where no particular measure word is given, students may assume 個 (ge) is to be used.

I

學生1　你有沒有毛筆？

學生2　沒有，我沒有毛筆。我有鋼筆，我有一枝很新的鋼筆。

學生1　你有沒有鉛筆？

學生2　有，我有三枝長的，兩枝短的。

學生1　你的那兩枝短鉛筆好不好？

學生2　不好，長鉛筆好，短鉛筆不好。

學生1　那本新書的紙好不好？

學生2　不好，很不好。

II

學生1　他們的黑板是新的，對不對？

學生2　對了，是新的。他們的那個大黑板很新。

學生1　那個新黑板乾淨不乾淨？

學生2　乾淨，他們的那個新黑板很乾淨。

學生1　你們的那個本子是不是新的？

學生2　不是，是舊的。

學生1　你們沒〔有〕新本子，對不對？

學生2　不，我們有新本子，我們有很多新本子。

III

　　張老師有很多好朋友，他們是英國人，他們有很多英文書，英文報。張老師是中國人，他有中文報，沒有英文報。

LESSON IV

New Words (traditional characters)

1.	工作	v	gōngzuò	to work
2.	只	adv	zhǐ	only
3.	學習	v	xuéxí	to study, learn
4.	看	v	kàn	to read, look at
5.	嘸	int	ḿ	what (did you say)?
6.	呢	p	ne	question particle
7.	也	adv	yě	too, also
8.	幾	nu	jǐ	how many, a few
9.	二	nu	èr	two
10.	四	nu	sì	four
11.	五	nu	wǔ	five
12.	六	nu	liù	six
13.	教	v	jiāo	to teach
14.	多少	nu	duōshǎo	how many?
15.	十	nu	shí	ten
16.	七	nu	qī	seven
17.	八	nu	bā	eight
18.	九	nu	jiǔ	nine
19.	給	v	gěi	to give
20.	謝謝	v	xièxie	thank you

I

學生1	你工作不工作？
學生2	不工作。我只學習，我學習中文。
學生1	你看不看中文報？
學生2	嗯？
學生1	你看中文報不看？
學生2	不看。
學生1	你朋友呢？
學生2	他也不看。我們只看中文書。
學生1	你們有幾本中文書？
學生2	有...一本，兩本，三本，四本，五本，六本...有六本。
學生1	幾本新的？幾本舊的？
學生2	兩本新的，四本舊的。

II

學生1	張老師教你不教？
學生2	教，他教我中文。他是（一）個很好的老師。
學生1	他只教中國學生嗎？
學生2	不，他也教美國人。
學生1	他教多少學生？
學生2	他教三十七個學生。
學生1	他教多少美國學生？多少中國學生？
學生2	他教二十八個美國學生，九個中國學生。
學生1	你們（的）老師給你們本子不給？
學生2	不給。我們有本子，一個人有一個本子。

III

朋友1	你好嗎？
朋友2	好，我很好。謝謝。你呢？
朋友1	我也很好，謝謝。

New Words (traditional characters)

1.	把	m	bǎ	measure word
2.	椅子	n	yǐzi	chair
3.	和	conj	hé	and
4.	桌子	n	zhuōzi	table, desk
5.	都	adv	dōu	all
6.	些	m	xiē	a few, some
7.	學校	n	xuéxiào	school
8.	人民	n	rénmín	people
9.	日報	n	rìbào	daily (newspaper)
10.	畫報	n	huàbào	pictorial
11.	有意思	adj	yǒuyìsi	interesting
12.	學	v	xué	to learn (a skill), to study (a subject)
13.	日語	n	Rìyǔ	Japanese language
14.	還是	conj	háishi	--- or ---
15.	漢語	n	Hànyǔ	Chinese language
16.	會	v	huì	to know how, to be skillful in...
17.	作	v	zuò	to do (exercise), to make
18.	練習	n, v	liànxì	exercise, to practice
19.	用	v	yòng	to use

I

朋友1	那兩把椅子和那張桌子都是你的嗎？
朋友2	不。這些都不是我的，都是學校的。
朋友1	你沒有桌子和椅子嗎？
朋友2	沒有。桌子和椅子我都沒有。
朋友1	那些人民日報和人民畫報呢？也都是學校的嗎？
朋友2	不都是。這些人民畫報是我的。
朋友1	人民畫報有意思還是人民日報有意思？
朋友2	人民畫報有意思。

II

中國朋友	你學日語還是學漢語？
美國朋友	我都學。我學一些日語，也學一些漢語。
中國朋友	毛美文呢？他也都學嗎？
美國朋友	不，他只學日語，不學漢語，他會漢語。
中國朋友	你們作練習不作？
美國朋友	作，我們作很多練習。
中國朋友	你們用鋼筆（還是）用鉛筆？
美國朋友	鉛筆，鋼筆我們都用。

New Words (traditional characters)

1.	貴姓		guìxìng	(What's your) honorable surname?
2.	姓	v, n	xìng	to have the surname of..., surname
3.	叫	v	jiào	to be called, to call
4.	甚麼	p	shénme	what?
5.	名字	n	míngzi	name (full or first)
6.	怎麼	adv	zěnme	how? why?
7.	以前	adv	yǐqián	formerly
8.	怎麼樣		zěnmeyàng	how about...?
9.	吧	par	ba	suggestion particle
10.	位	m	wèi	M for people
11.	知道	v	zhīdao	to know (about a fact)
12.	山本	n	Shānběn	Yamamoto (Japanese surname)
13.	哪	sp	nǎ/něi	which?
14.	第	pref	dì	ordinal prefix
15.	日本	n	Rìběn	Japan
16.	誰	p	shéi	who?
17.	跟	conj	gēn	and
18.	同屋	n	tóngwū	roommate
19.	懂	v	dǒng	understand
20.	大學	n	dàxué	university, college

Text (traditional characters)

I

毛美文　您貴姓？
謝新民　我姓謝，我叫謝新民。你叫甚麼名字？
　毛　我叫毛美文。我的英文名字叫Marion Mudd。中國朋友都叫我毛美文。
　謝　你怎麼有中文名字？
　毛　我以前學習漢語，我們的老師給我們中文名字。
　謝　你（的）這個名字很好。我也叫你毛美文，怎麼樣？
　毛　好。我叫你甚麼呢？
　謝　朋友都叫我小謝，你也叫我小謝吧！

II

　謝　那三位老師都姓甚麼？你知道不知道？
　毛　我知道。一個姓張，一個姓毛，一個姓山本。
　謝　哪位姓張？
　毛　第一位姓張。
　謝　第二位呢？
　毛　第二位姓毛。
　謝　山本老師是日本人吧？
　毛　對了，他是日本人，他教日語。
　謝　他教誰日語？
　毛　他教新學生日語。
　謝　誰教你跟你同屋呢？

- 13 -

毛　張老師教我們。

謝　你的日語怎麼樣？

毛　不很好，懂一些。

謝　這個大學的學生都學習日語嗎？

毛　不，不都學；很多人學漢語。

New Words (traditional characters)

1.	年	n	nián	year
2.	忙	adj	máng	busy
3.	月	n	yuè	month
4.	今年	n	jīnnián	this year
5.	去	v	qù	to go
6.	今天	n	jīntian	today
7.	來	v	lái	to come
8.	星期	n	xīngqī	week
9.	日	n	rì	day
10.	點(鐘)	m	diǎn (zhōng)	o'clock (point on the clock)
11.	過	v	guò	to pass (time)
12.	刻	m	kè	quarter (of an hour)
13.	現在	n	xiànzài	now
14.	時候(兒)	n	shíhou(r)	time
15.	差	v	chà	to be short of
16.	分	n	fēn	minute
17.	半	m	bàn	half
18.	號	n	hào	ordinal day of month
19.	天	n	tiān	day
20.	零	nu	líng	zero

I

謝新民　你一年都很忙，對不對？
毛美文　不。我七月，八月，九月都不忙。
謝　　今年你去不去中國？
毛　　今年不去。
謝　　你哪年去？
毛　　我一九＿＿*年六月去。

II

毛　　你朋友今天來不來？
謝　　今天（是）星期幾？
毛　　星期三。
謝　　今天他來。他星期一，（星期）三，（星期）五都來。
毛　　星期日呢？
謝　　星期日他不來。
毛　　他幾點鐘來？
謝　　他九點過一刻來。現在（是）甚麼時候兒？
毛　　現在九點差五分。

III

朋友1　這些都是哪年的報？
朋友2　一些是這半年的，一些是一九八二年的。
朋友1　你有沒有今年四月三號跟六號的報？
朋友2　沒有，我沒有那兩天的報。

――――――

*Speaker may supply any number to make this a future year.

LESSON VIII

New Words (traditional characters)

1.	上午	n	shàngwǔ	morning
2.	到	fv	dào	(to go) to (a place)
3.	哪兒(哪裡)p		nǎr (nǎli)	where
4.	那兒(那裡)p		nàr (nàli)	there
5.	在	v	zài	to be at a place
6.	宿舍	n	sùshè	dormitory
7.	一起	adv	yīqǐ	together
8.	喜歡	v	xǐhuan	to like
9.	電影(兒)	n	diànyǐng(r)	movie
10.	下午	n	xiàwǔ	afternoon
11.	要	v	yào	to want to
12.	但是	conj	dànshi	but
13.	跟	fv	gēn	with
14.	從	fv	cóng	from
15.	這兒(這裡)p		zhèr (zhèli)	here
16.	有事兒	adj	yǒushèr	not free, busy
17.	爲甚麼	adv	wèishénme	why
18.	問	v	wèn	to ask (a question)
19.	前天	n	qiántiān	day before yesterday

I

小張　你上午到哪兒去？

毛美文　我到我朋友那兒去。

　張　你朋友在哪兒？

　毛　在宿舍。

　張　我上午也去宿舍。我們一起去，好嗎？

　毛　好。

II

小張　你喜歡看電影嗎？

毛美文　喜歡，很喜歡。

　張　你看不看今天下午的日本電影？

　毛　要看，但是不知道怎麼去。

　張　我知道。你跟我去。兩點半從我這兒去，怎麼樣？

　毛　兩點半我在小謝那兒。我們從小謝那兒去，好不好？

　張　小謝也跟我們一起去嗎？

　毛　不，他不去，他三點半有事兒。你為甚麼問？

　張　他不去看電影兒，你為甚麼要從他那兒去呢？

　毛　我要看前天的那張中文報。那張報在他那兒。我一點鐘要到他那兒去。

　張　好。我兩點半到小謝那兒去。

New Words (traditional characters)

1.	外邊(兒)	n	wàibian(r)	outside
2.	好看	adj	hǎokàn	good-looking
3.	裡邊(兒)	n	lǐbian(r)	inside
4.	舒服	adj	shūfu	comfortable
5.	自學	v	zìxué	to self-study, to do homework
6.	圖書館	n	túshūguǎn	library
7.	常常*	adv	chángcháng	frequently, most of the time
8.	雜誌	n	zázhì	magazine
9.	地方	n	dìfang	place
10.	前邊(兒)	n	qiánbian(r)	front
11.	後邊(兒)	n	hòubian(r)	back
12.	左邊(兒)	n	zuǒbian(r)	left side
13.	右邊(兒)	n	yòubian(r)	right side
14.	上邊(兒)	n	shàngbian(r)	top, above
15.	旁邊(兒)	n	pángbiān(r)	side
16.	下邊(兒)	n	xiàbian(r)	bottom, below
17.	中間(兒)	n	zhōngjiàn(r)	middle, between, among
18.	有時候(兒)	adv	yǒushíhou(r)	sometimes
19.	她	p	tā	she, her

---

*may be shortened to 常 (cháng).

I

毛美文　我的宿舍很好。外邊兒很好看。裡邊兒很乾淨，很舒服。
　小謝　你常常在宿舍〔裡〕自學嗎？
　　毛　不。我常在圖書館〔裡〕自學。那兒書多，雜誌也多。
　　謝　你們的圖書館在甚麼地方？
　　毛　大的在宿舍前邊兒，小的在宿舍後邊兒。
　　謝　你去哪個？
　　毛　我常去宿舍後邊兒的那個。

II

　　謝　哪張桌子是你的？
　　毛　左邊兒的那張。右邊兒的那張是我同屋的。
　　謝　你的桌子上有很多書。爲甚麼她的桌子上沒有書？
　　毛　她不喜歡桌子上邊兒有書。你看，她的書在椅子下邊兒，椅子旁邊兒。
　　謝　你們的兩張桌子中間兒也有很多書。那些書是誰的？
　　毛　也是她的。我的書都在桌子上。

III

　　謝　一年有十二個月，半年有六個月。
　　毛　對了，半年有六個月。
　　謝　一個月有三十一天。
　　毛　不對，不對！有時候只有三十天。二月常常只有二十八天。
　　謝　今年的二月有多少天？
　　毛　有二十九天。

LESSON X

New Words (traditional characters)

1.	念書	v-o	niànshū	to study
2.	得	par	de	verb particle
3.	高興	adj	gāoxìng	cheerful, glad
4.	特別	adj, adv	tèbié	special, unusually
5.	看書	v-o	kànshū	to read (silently)
6.	寫字	v-o	xiězì	to write
7.	快	adj	kuài	fast
8.	慢	adj	màn	slow
9.	說話	v-o	shuōhuà	to speak, to talk
10.	太	adv	tài	too (much)
11.	自己	p, adv	zìjǐ	oneself, by oneself
12.	積極	adj	jījí	positive, enthusiastic
13.	唱歌(兒)	v-o	chànggē(r)	to sing
14.	跳舞	v-o	tiàowǔ	to dance
15.	一定	adv	yīdìng	definitely, certainly
16.	國歌(兒)	n	guógē(r)	national anthem
17.	教書	v-o	jiāoshū	to teach

I

高文　你在這兒念書念得怎麼樣？

小張　念得很高興。我特別喜歡學漢語。

高　　你喜歡看書還是寫字？

張　　我喜歡寫字。

高　　你現在寫得快不快？

張　　不快，我寫得很慢。我說話也說得很慢。老師常說我們說話說得太慢。

高　　我的日語老師也說我們〔說話〕說得太慢。是不是他們自己說得太快？

張　　你說得很對。他們有時候兒也太積極，是不是？

II

毛美文　你是不是喜歡唱歌，跳舞？

謝新民　我喜歡唱歌，不喜歡跳舞。

毛　　他們都跟我說你唱歌唱得很好。

謝　　哪裡！我唱得不好，但是喜歡唱。你們美國人一定都喜歡跳舞，是不是？

毛　　不一定，不都喜歡，但是我很喜歡。我常常跟朋友一起跳舞。我也喜歡唱歌兒。你教我一兩個中國歌兒，好不好？

謝　　好，你要學甚麼歌兒吧？

毛　　你教我你們的國歌兒吧！

LESSON XI

New Words (traditional characters)

1.	了	par	le		completion particle
2.	這麼	adv	zènme		so, this way
3.	晚	adj	wǎn		late
4.	昨天	n	zuótiān		yesterday
5.	已經	adv	yǐjǐng		already
6.	早	adj	zǎo		early
7.	那麼	adv	nènme		that way
8.	才	adv	cái		not...until, belatedly
9.	年級	n	niánjí		year (class in school)
10.	下	pref	xià		next
11.	學期	n	xuéqī		school term
12.	開始	v	kāishǐ		to begin
13.	參加	v	cānjiā		to participate
14.	晚會	n	wǎnhuì		evening party
15.	吃	v	chī		to eat
16.	東西	n	dōngxi		thing
17.	玩兒	v	wár		to play, to have fun
18.	還	adv	hái		yet, in addition to
*19.	哈佛	n	Hǎfó		Harvard

---

*An asterisk before a word in the table of new words indicates that the item appears in the pattern sentences of the <u>Companion Book</u>.

I

小謝　今天的報來了沒有？

小張　還沒〔有〕來呢！

　謝　今天爲甚麼來得這麼晚？昨天這〔個〕時候兒已經來了，是不是？

　張　今天是星期二。星期一，三，五來得早，二，四，六來得晚。

　謝　那麼星期日呢？

　張　星期日也來得很晚。有時候十點半才來。

II

　謝　你們學了寫字沒有？

　張　還沒學呢！

　謝　小高他們已經學了，你們爲甚麼還沒學呢？

　張　他們是二年級的，我們是一年級的。

　謝　你們甚麼時候兒才學呢？

　張　我們下〔個〕學期開始。

III

高文　你參加了前天的晚會沒有？

小張　〔我〕沒有〔參加〕。你們呢？

　高　我們去了。很有意思。

　張　你們跳了舞沒有？

　高　我跳了，我跳了兩個舞。她沒跳，她跟朋友們說了很多話。
　　　我們還吃了不少東西，玩兒得很高興。

LESSON XII

New Words (traditional characters)

1.	遇見	v	yùjian		to meet someone (by chance)
2.	大家	p	dàjiā		all, everybody
3.	哦	int	ò		oh
4.	認識	v	rènshi		to recognize, to be acquainted with
5.	聽	v	tīng		to listen
6.	不錯	adj	bùcuò		pretty good
7.	句	m	jù		M for sentences
8.	就	adv	jiù		then
9.	走	v	zǒu		to go away, to walk
10.	明天	n	míngtiān		tomorrow
11.	晚上	n	wǎnshang		evening
12.	晚飯	n	wǎnfàn		evening meal
13.	句子	n	jùzi		sentence
14.	講	v	jiǎng		to explain
15.	清楚	adj	qīngchu		clear
16.	復習	v	fùxí		to review
17.	語法	n	yǔfǎ		grammar
18.	課文	n	kèwén	(課)	text
19.	生詞	n	shēngcí		vocabulary (new word)
*20.	念	v	niàn		to read out loud

I

常學思　毛美文來了沒有？

小張　　還沒〔來〕呢！她兩點半來。現在才兩點過五分，是不是？

常　　　對。我昨天在她那兒遇見了一個中國人。

張　　　那個人叫甚麼名字？

常　　　我沒有問他。大家都叫他小謝。

張　　　哦，你遇見了謝新民。我認識他。他唱歌兒唱得很好。你們聽了他唱歌兒沒有？

常　　　聽了。昨天他唱了三個歌兒，都唱得很不錯。

張　　　你跟他説了話沒有？

常　　　只説了兩句話。他很忙，唱了歌兒就走了。

張　　　我很喜歡跟他説話。明天晚上吃了晚飯我就到他那兒去，跟他説説話。你去不去？

常　　　去。我也去看看他。

II

常學思　今天的練習有八個句子，你作了幾個了？

小張　　〔我〕作了四個了。

常　　　你會作後邊兒的那四個嗎？

張　　　老師講得很清楚，我會作。我現在復習復習生詞。復習了生詞就作那些句子。

常　　　你今天也復習語法和課文嗎？

張　　　也復習。作了那些句子就復習語法和課文。

LESSON XIII

New Words (traditional characters)

1.	會	op	huì	can, likely to (could)
2.	漢字	n	Hànzì	Chinese characters
3.	沒關係		méiguānxi	(it) does not matter
4.	以後	adv	yǐhòu	in the future
5.	得	op	děi	to have to
6.	字典	n	zìdiǎn	dictionary
7.	能	op	néng	can
8.	想	op	xiǎng	to wish to, to think
9.	打	v	dǎ	to play, to hit
10.	球	n	qiú	ball
11.	後天	n	hòutian	day after tomorrow
12.	考試	n, v	kǎoshì	examination, test
13.	準備	v	zhǔnbèi	to prepare
14.	應該	op	yīnggāi	should
15.	努力	adj	nǔlì	diligent
16.	辦法	n	bànfa	way (to deal with difficulty)
17.	非常	adv	fēicháng	extremely, very (much)
18.	可以	op	kěyǐ	may
19.	找	v	zhǎo	to look for, to seek...out
20.	地	par	de	structural particle
21.	不用	op	bùyòng	don't have to

Text (traditional characters)

I

小謝　你現在會不會寫漢字？

小張　會，但是寫得很慢，也寫得不好看。

　謝　沒關係，以後會寫得很好看。

　張　老師也這麼說。我要好好兒地練習練習。

　謝　你聽得快不快？

　張　還聽得很慢。老師還得說得很慢。

　謝　你們會用字典不會？

　張　不會，現在還不會，以後要慢慢兒地學。現在只要能聽，能說，能看，能寫。

II

高文　你想不想去打球？

小張　我很想打球，但是今天不能打。

　高　為甚麼呢？

　張　下午得好好兒地念書。後天有個日語考試，我得準備準備。

　高　我們不應該太努力，有時候兒也該玩兒玩兒。

　張　你說得很對，但是有甚麼辦法呢？

　高　我有個好辦法：我有個日本朋友非常喜歡打球。我們可以找他跟我們一起打球，我們也可以跟他練習練習日語。

　張　這個辦法不錯。他會不會太忙，不能來？

　高　我們去找找他。

LESSON XIV

New Words (traditional characters)

1.	同學	n	tóngxué	schoolmate
2.	演	v	yǎn	to act, to present (a play)
3.	話劇	n	huàjù	play
4.	注意	v	zhùyì	to pay attention to
5.	上	pref	shàng	previous, last
6.	通知	n	tōngzhī	notice
7.	因為...所以	conj	yīnwèi...suǒyǐ	because...therefore
8.	交	v	jiāo	to hand in
9.	報告	n	bàogào	report
10.	別的	p	biéde	others
11.	事情	n	shìqing　(件)	matter, affair
12.	家	n	jiā	family, home
13.	有名	adj	yǒumíng	famous
14.	不停地	adv	bùtíngde	unceasingly
15.	鼓掌	v	gǔzhǎng	to clap hands
16.	休息	v	xiūxi	to rest
17.	重要	adj	zhòngyào	important
18.	掌握	v	zhǎngwò	to master, to understand thoroughly
19.	意思	n	yìsi	meaning
20.	討論	v	tǎolùn	to discuss

高文　你看了同學們前天演的那個話劇沒有？

張力　甚麼話劇？

高　　你沒有注意他們上星期給我們的那個通知吧？

張　　我這兩天因爲要交一個報告，所以很忙，沒有注意別的事情。他們演的話劇叫甚麼名字？

高　　叫"家"。

張　　這個話劇很有名。他們演得怎麼樣？

高　　非常好。大家看了以後都不停地鼓掌。你的報告交了沒有？

張　　還沒呢！明天可以交。沒寫以前不知道要用這麼多時候兒。

高　　明天你交了報告以後，應該休息休息。

張　　我也想休息休息，但是我還得作那個日語練習呢！很多重要的地方我還沒有掌握，可以問你嗎？

高　　可以。有一兩個句子的意思我也不清楚，我們一起討論討論吧！

LESSON XV

New Words (traditional characters)

1.	買	v	mǎi	to buy
2.	漢英	n	Hàn-Yīng	Chinese-English
3.	當然	adv	dāngrán	of course
4.	拿	v	ná	to take, to pick up
5.	種	m	zhǒng	kind
6.	有用	adj	yǒuyòng	useful
7.	合作社	n	hézuòshè	co-op
8.	賣	v	mài	sell
9.	每	sp	měi	each, every
10.	上課	v-o	shàngkè	to attend/to hold a class
11.	從...到	mk	cóng...dào	from...to
12.	就	adv	jiù	(already)
13.	問題	n	wèntí	question
14.	回答	v	huídá	to answer
15.	有的	p	yǒude	some
16.	怎麼辦		zěnmebàn	What is there to do?
17.	告訴	v	gàosu	to tell (a person)
18.	必須	op	bìxū	should, must
19.	互相	adv	hùxiāng	mutually
20.	要是...就	conj	yàoshi...jiù...	if...then...
21.	方法	n	fāngfǎ	method, way (of doing things)

I

毛美文　你昨天買的那本漢英字典，我可以看看嗎？

張力　　當然可以。在桌子上。你自己拿吧！

毛　　　（看字典）這種字典很有用。我也應該有一本。

張　　　你要是想買，就得快快兒地去買。合作社裡的人說，現在買這種字典的人很多。

毛　　　我不想買新的。這兒有沒有賣舊字典的地方？

張　　　我不知道。你可以問問小謝，他知道很多賣舊書的地方。

II

小謝　　他們每天甚麼時候兒上中文課？

張力　　他們從一點過五分到兩點上中文課。

謝　　　他們甚麼時候兒才開始說話？

張　　　他們已經開始了，他們九月就開始了。

謝　　　上課的時候兒，他們能說中國話嗎？

張　　　能說。老師問問題，他們回答。

謝　　　老師問的問題，他們都能回答嗎？

張　　　有的他們能回答，有的他們不能回答。

謝　　　要是不能回答，怎麼辦呢？

張　　　要是他們不能回答，他們的老師就告訴他們。

謝　　　每個學生老師都問嗎？

張　　　都問。每個人都必須回答。

謝　　　學生們自己也互相問問題嗎？

張　　　有時候兒互相問問題，有時候兒一起討論課文裡的意思，這是學習的好方法。

LESSON XVI

New Words (traditional characters)

1.	課本	n	kèběn			textbook
2.	着	v	zháo			to reach (as RC)
3.	剛	adv	gāng			just
4.	完	v	wán			to finish
5.	東方	n	dōngfāng			east, eastern
6.	書店	n	shūdiàn	(家，個)		bookstore
7.	也許	adv	yěxǔ			maybe
8.	看見	v	kànjian			to see
9.	開會	v-o	kāihuì			to hold a meeting
10.	請	v	qǐng			to ask, to invite
11.	當	v	dāng			to be, to act as
12.	主席	n	zhǔxí			chairperson
13.	件	m	jiàn			measure word
14.	聽見	v	tīngjian			to hear
15.	別人	p	biérén			others (other people)
16.	水平	n	shuǐpīng			level of proficiency
17.	低	adj	dī			low
18.	行	v	xíng			to be good enough, will do
*19.	高	adj	gāo			high

I

張力1　字典和漢語課本都買着了嗎？

毛美文1　課本買着了，字典沒買着。我去得太完了，他們剛賣完。

張力2　你可以到東方書店去看看，那兒也許有。

毛美文2　好，我作完練習就去。

II

高文1　你今天看見了毛美文沒有？

張力1　沒有。你要找她嗎？

高2　對了。我要問她一件事，下（個）星期開討論會，我想問她能不能當主席。

張2　上星期我聽見她跟別人說她每天三點鐘以後，都在合作社工作。你要是去那兒，一定可以找着她。

高3　我昨天去了，但是沒找着她。合作社的人說她昨天沒去。

張3　毛美文也許太忙。你爲甚麼一定要找她當主席呢？你自己當吧！

高4　我的日文水平太低。你來，怎麼樣？

張4　我也不行。還是請毛美文好。

New Words (traditional characters)

1.	站	v	zhàn	to stand
2.	門口(兒)	n	ménkǒu(r)	entrance, doorway
3.	坐	v	zuò	to sit
4.	熱	adj	rè	hot
5.	覺得	v	juéde	to feel
6.	有(一)點兒	adv	yǒu(yi)diǎr	somewhat
7.	頭	n	tóu	head
8.	疼	v	téng	to ache
9.	臉	n	liǎn	face
10.	紅	adj	hóng	red
11.	開	v	kāi	open
12.	窗户	n	chuānghu	window
13.	試	v	shì	to try
14.	壞	adj	huài	bad, broken, out of order
15.	差不多	adv	chàbuduō	almost
16.	完全	adv	wánquán	completely
17.	看	v	kàn	(It) depends (on)
18.	幾	nu	jǐ	a few, some
19.	借	v	jiè	to borrow, to lend
20.	成	v	chéng	to succeed (in) to become
21.	極了	inten	jíle	extremely

I

張力　你爲甚麼要站在門口兒？

小謝　我坐的地方太熱了。我覺得有〔一〕點兒不舒服，有〔一〕點
　　　兒頭疼。

　張　你的臉很紅。你爲甚麼不開開窗户呢？

　謝　我試了，但是開不開，也許壞了。

　張　我這兒不熱，你要不要坐到這兒來？

　謝　可以嗎？我可以坐在你旁邊兒的那把椅子上嗎？

　張　當然可以，我拿開我的東西。

II

高文　你那個報告今天寫得完寫不完？

張力　差不多寫好了，現在完全要看今天上午看得見看不見毛美文了。

　高　爲甚麼呢？

　張　我要在報告裡寫幾個漢字，想借毛美文的那枝好毛筆。要是看不
　　　見毛美文，當然就借不到毛筆。要是借不到毛筆，那幾個漢字就
　　　寫不成，這個報告也就寫不完了。

　高　你看，毛美文來了。

　張　好極了。我這個報告今天寫得完了。

LESSON XVIII

New Words (traditional characters)

1.	回	v	huí		to return
2.	收音機	n	shōuyīnjī	(架，個)	radio
3.	帶	v	dài		to bring along
4.	進	v	jìn		to enter
5.	搬	v	bān		to move
					(one's residence)
6.	間	m	jiān		M for rooms
7.	屋子	n	wūzi	(間)	room
8.	歡迎	v	huānyíng		to welcome
9.	山	n	shān	(座)	hill, mountain
10.	便宜	adj	piányi		inexpensive
11.	城(裡)	n	chéng(li)		(in the) city
12.	公共汽車	n	gōnggòngqìchē	(輛)	bus (public car)
13.	費	v	fèi		to take a lot
					(money, time)
14.	時間	n	shíjiān		time
15.	出	v	chū		to go out
16.	倒是	adv	dàoshi		admittedly so
17.	方便	adj	fāngbiàn		convenient
18.	騎	v	qí		to sit astride
19.	自行車	n	zìxíngchē	(輛)	bicycle
*20.	輛	m	liàng		M for vehicles

張力　毛美文，你回來了。收音機買來了沒有？

毛美文　買來了。還帶來了一個人。你看，誰進來了？

張力　小謝！你怎麼來了？

謝新民　我在店裡遇見了毛美文。她告訴我你們這兒有一個人搬走了。我想搬來，所以來看看那間屋子。

張　好。我帶你去看看。

（張和謝看了屋子以後回來了。）

毛　怎麼樣？你喜歡嗎？

謝　那間屋子小是小，但是很乾淨。我非常喜歡。我想下月一號就搬來，行不行？

張　當然行。歡迎你搬來。但是你山上的那個地方很大很便宜，你為甚麼要搬到城裡來呢？

謝　那個地方好是好，但是我每天得坐公共汽車來上課，很費時間，所以想搬到這兒來。

張　這兒出來進去倒是方便。

謝　你們每天怎麼去學校？是騎自行車去還是走去？

毛　我走去，小張騎自行車去。

LESSON XIX

New Words (traditional characters)

1.	啊	int	ā	ah!
2.	就是	v	jiùshi	to be exactly
3.	談話	v	tánhuà	to talk, to converse
4.	住	v	zhù	to live, to stay
5.	台北	n	Táiběi	Taipei
6.	忘	v	wàng	to forget
7.	到	v	dào	to reach, to arrive
8.	習慣	v, n	xíguàn	to be used to, habit, custom
9.	父親	n	fùqin	father
10.	母親	n	mǔqin	mother
11.	哥哥	n	gēge	elder brother
12.	弟弟	n	dìdi	younger brother
13.	姐姐	n	jiějie	elder sister
14.	妹妹	n	mèimei	younger sister
15.	父母	n	fùmǔ	parents
16.	大夫	n	dàifu	doctor
17.	教師	n	jiàoshī	teacher (as a profession)
18.	剛才	adv	gāngcái	a moment ago
19.	客氣	adj	kèqi	polite, modest
20.	樓	m	lóu	(nth) floor (in a building)

高文遇見了謝新民

高　你是從中國來的嗎？

謝　是。我是兩個月以前才從北京來的。

高　我叫高文。高興的高，中文的文。你叫甚麼名字？

謝　我姓謝，我叫謝新民。

高　啊！你就是小謝！毛美文談話的時候兒常常談到你。你也住在這兒嗎？

謝　對了，我是昨天晚上才搬來的。你的中國話說得很好，是在這個大學學的嗎？

高　不是，是三年前在台北學的，已經忘了不少了。你喜歡美國嗎？

謝　剛到的時候兒很不習慣，現在好了。

高　你家裡有幾個人？

謝　我家（裡）有父親，母親，一個哥哥，一個弟弟。

高　沒有姐姐，妹妹嗎？

謝　沒有。

高　你父母工作不工作？

謝　都工作。我父親是大夫，我母親是英文教師。

高　剛才我聽見你英文說得很好，現在我知道為甚麼了。你是跟你母親學的英文吧？

謝　不是。我是在北（京）大（學）學的。我說得不好，還得跟你們學習。

高　你太客氣。我們以後可以常常談話了。你住在幾樓？

謝　我住在四樓，你呢？

高　我住在二樓。

LESSON XX

New Words (traditional characters)

1.	打	v	dǎ	to hit, to strike
2.	電話	n	diànhuà	telephone
3.	喂	int	wèi	hello!
4.	奇怪	adv	qíguài	strange, feel strange
5.	叫	v	jiào	to order someone to, to ask
6.	對不起	v	duìbuqǐ	I am sorry
7.	發燒	v-o	fāshāo	to run a temperature
8.	一點兒	m	yīdiǎr	a little
9.	感冒	v	gǎnmào	to have a cold
10.	藥	n	yào	medicine
11.	片(兒)	m	piàn(r)	a piece
12.	止痛片	n	zhǐtòngpiàn	analgesic tablet (aspirin)
13.	病	v, n	bìng	to be sick; illness
14.	發展	v	fāzhǎn	to develop
15.	醫院	n	yīyuàn	hospital
16.	走路	v-o	zǒulù	to walk
17.	了	v	liǎo	to be able to
18.	開車	v-o	kāichē	to drive (a car)
19.	再見	v	zàijiàn	(to see you again) goodbye
20.	一會兒	n	yīhuǐr	in a moment

打電話

張力	喂，小謝在嗎？我要找小謝說話。
謝新民	我就是。你是小張吧！有甚麼事情？
張	今天上午你沒有來唱歌，大家都很奇怪，叫我打電話來問問你。
謝	我今天頭疼，所以沒去。對不起！
張	你發燒不發燒？
謝	我有一點兒燒。我想我感冒了。
張	你吃了藥沒有？
謝	我吃了兩片止痛片，但是沒有用。
張	你應該看看大夫。
謝	感冒是小病，在家裡休息休息就可以了。
張	不，感冒有時候兒會發展成大病，特別是有燒的時候兒。
謝	我不認識大夫，怎麼辦呢？
張	學校的醫院大夫很多很好。你可以到那兒去看看。
謝	我現在頭疼，走不了路，還是在家休息休息吧！
張	我開車帶你去。我五分鐘以後就來，好嗎？
謝	好吧！謝謝你了。
張	沒關係，不謝。再見，一會兒見。

LESSON XXI

New Words (traditional characters)

1.	給	fv	gěi		for, to
2.	信	n	xìn	(封)	letter
3.	病人	n	bìngrén		patient
4.	或者	conj	huòzhě		(either)...or
5.	多	nu	duō		an indefinite number
6.	熱情	adj	rèqíng		warm, compassionate
7.	對	prep	duì		to, towards
8.	還	v	huán		to return (things borrowed)
9.	並且	conj	bìngqiě		also, as well
10.	替	fv	tì		for
11.	送	v	sòng		to take...to a place
12.	決定	v	juédìng		to decide
13.	搞	v	gǎo		to engage in, to do
14.	小説(兒)	n	xiǎoshuō(r)		novel
15.	一史	suf	--shǐ		history of...
16.	翻譯	v	fānyì		to translate
17.	冷	adj	lěng		cold
18.	希望	v	xīwàng		to hope
19.	身體	n	shēntǐ		health, body
20.	祝	v	zhù		to wish (you...)

大哥：
三弟：

　　很長時間沒有給你們寫信了。你們都好吧？

　　上星期我病了，住了四天的醫院。回來以後休息了兩天。今天覺得差不多好了。明天或者後天可以上課了。

　　這兩個多月裡，我認識了十多個美國朋友。他們都很熱情，都對我很好。我在醫院裡的時候兒，他們每天都去看我，並且給我作很多事情，替我買東西，替我還書。進醫院的時候兒，也是他們送我去的。

　　我已經決定搞美國小說史了。這兒的圖書館新書很多，雜誌也多，非常方便。

　　父親母親都好嗎？父親的病人多不多？母親的英文小說翻譯好了沒有？

　　現在冷了，希望大家注意身體，並且常常寫信！

　　祝

好！

　　　　　　　　　　　　　　　　　　　新民
　　　　　　　　　　　　　　　　　　　一月十號

LESSON XXII

New Words (traditional characters)

1.	過	v	guò		to pass by (a suffix)
2.	就要...了		jiùyào...le		about to...
3.	春節	n	chūnjié		spring festival
4.	它	p	tā		it
5.	一樣	v	yīyàng		to be the same
6.	像	adj	xiàng		to resemble
7.	聖誕節	n	Shèngdànjié		Christmas
8.	放假	v	fàngjià		to have vacation
9.	兒女	n	érnǚ		children (of parents)
10.	別	op	bié		don't...
11.	錯	v	cuò		to be wrong
12.	請	v	qǐng		to ask
13.	次	m	cì		time (M for episodes)
14.	筷子	n	kuàizi		chopsticks
15.	難	adj	nán		difficult
16.	餓	adj	è		hungry
17.	家	m	jiā		M for business operations
18.	飯館兒	n	fànguǎn(r)	(家)	restaurant
19.	菜	n	cài		dish (cooked)
20.	南方	n	nánfāng		southern

Text (traditional characters)

I

小張　時間過得很快。二月就要來了。今年的第一個月已經要過完了。

小謝　對了，春節也快要到了。

張　甚麼是春節？

謝　春節就是中國的舊新年。我們也叫它春節。

張　春節是幾月幾號？

謝　每年都不一樣。今年是二月四號。

張　中國人怎麼過春節？

謝　像你們過聖誕節一樣。那天每個地方都放假，兒女們都到父母家去，大家都高高興興地玩兒一天，吃一天。

張　春節那天我看見中國人的時候兒應該說甚麼？

謝　你可以說，"春節好！"也可以說，"祝你春節好。"

張　"春節好…祝你春節好。"我得好好兒地練習練習，四號那天別說錯了。

II

謝新民　下星期六是春節，我準備請你在中國城吃飯。你在中國城吃過飯嗎？

高文　吃過一次，並且是用筷子吃的。

謝　用筷子吃中國飯難不難？

高　不難，我用過很多次，但是太餓的時候兒我不用。

謝　你去的那家飯館叫甚麼名字？菜好不好？

高　是一個南方飯館，菜很不錯。名字我忘了。

LESSON XXIII

New Words (traditional characters)

1.	正	adv	zhèng		progressive expression: happen to be
2.	天氣	n	tiānqì		weather
3.	暖和	adj	nuǎnhe		warm
4.	穿	v	chuān		to wear, to put on
5.	着	par	zhe		--ing
6.	大衣	n	dàyī	（件）	overcoat
7.	冬天	n	dōngtiān		winter
8.	真	adv, adj	zhēn		really, real
9.	比	fv	bǐ		than, compare
10.	讓	fv	ràng		let, make
11.	下雪	v-o	xiàxuě		to snow
12.	刮風	v-o	guāfēng		to blow (wind)
13.	春天	n	chūntiān		spring
14.	好像	adv	hǎoxiàng		(it) seems to be
15.	過去	v	guòqu		to go over, to pass by
16.	夏天	n	xiātiān		summer
17.	去年	n	qùnián		last year
18.	秋天	n	qiūtiān		autumn
19.	下雨	v-o	xiàyǔ		to rain
20.	漂亮	adj	piàoliang		pretty
21.	男	adj	nán		male
22.	女	adj	nǚ		female

Text (traditional characters)

I

謝新民　請進！
　高文　你正在忙嗎？
　　謝　沒有，我正在看這本翻譯小說兒呢！
　　高　今天天氣很暖和。要不要出去走走？
　　謝　好啊！我也正想出去看看呢！不是很暖和嗎？你爲甚麼還穿着大衣呢？
　　高　暖和是暖和，還沒有那麼暖和呢！

II

　　謝　這兒的冬天真不短啊！
　　高　北京的冬天沒有這兒這麼長吧？
　　謝　不，有時候兒也長極了。
　　高　下雪下得很多嗎？
　　謝　下雪下得不比這兒多，但是常刮大風。刮風的時候兒很不舒服。
　　高　春天怎麼樣？
　　謝　春天很短，有時候兒好像冬天才過去，夏天就來了。這兒夏天熱不熱？
　　高　不一定，有時候兒很熱。
　　謝　去年我來的時候兒，正是秋天，天氣真好。讓我覺得跟在北京一樣。
　　高　秋天要是不下雨，倒是很漂亮。你喜歡春天還是喜歡秋天？
　　謝　我喜歡秋天。

高　我跟你不一樣。我覺得春天比秋天好。èi，那邊兒站着的兩個人
　　是誰？
謝　你説的是那兩個男的嗎？
高　不，我説的是那邊兒（的）那兩個女的。一個好像是毛美文。我
　　們過去看看，好不好？
謝　好。

LESSON XXIV

New Words (traditional characters)

1.	同時	adv	tóngshí		simultaneously
2.	散步	v-o	sànbù		to take a walk
3.	介紹	v	jièshao		to introduce
4.	小姐	n	xiǎojiě(ᵛ)		Miss
5.	生活	n	shēnghuó		(daily) life, living
6.	比方說	conj	bǐfāngshuō		for instance
7.	認爲	v	rènwéi		to consider, to have a strong opinion of (think)
8.	感覺	v, n	gǎnjué		to feel, feeling
9.	立刻	adv	lìkè		right away
10.	街	n	jiē	（條）	street
11.	人口	n	rénkǒu		population
12.	...分之...	m	...fēnzhī...		...parts of...
13.	就是	conj	jiùshì		it's just that, only
14.	體重	n	tǐzhòng		body weight
15.	增加	v	zēngjiā		to increase
16.	從前	adv	cóngqián		formerly, before
17.	從...起	adv	cóng (TW) qǐ		since or beginning (time)
18.	發現	v	fāxiàn		to discover
19.	發生	v	fāshēng		to occur, to come up

Text (traditional characters)

高文，謝新民〔同時〕　毛美文！

毛美文　你們也在散步嗎？來，我給你們介紹介紹。這是高文，這是謝
　　　　新民。
　　　　我們都叫他小謝。這位是史家明小姐，兩個星期以前才從台北來
　　　　的，也是我剛認識的朋友。

高
謝　　〔同時〕　　　你好！
史

謝　你習慣不習慣這兒的生活？

史　已經很習慣了。台北很多地方像美國一樣。

高　我認為台北有很多地方跟美國不一樣。

史　當然不完全一樣。比方說，這兒走路的人比台北少。

謝　我剛來的時候兒，感〔覺〕到的第一件事情也是這個。覺得街上
　　的人比中國少得多。

史　美國的人口只有中國的四分之一。街上走路的人當然也比中國少
　　了。

毛　並且，美國人開車的時候兒比走路多。我們走路走得太少了。高
　　文，你這幾天怎麼樣？

高　別的都好，就是體重增加了不少，所以現在每天散步。

毛　你從前沒有體重的問題，現在怎麼有這個問題了？

高　現在吃得比以前多一點兒了。

毛　為甚麼呢？

高　從上月發現了一家中國飯館兒起，我就常常吃中國飯，問題立刻
　　就發生了。

謝　你為甚麼不少吃一點兒呢？

高　那就是我的問題啊！

LESSON XXV

New Words (traditional characters)

1.	最	adv	zuì		the most
2.	困難	n, adj	kùnnan		difficulty, difficult
3.	容易	adj	róngyi		easy
4.	記	v	jì		to remember, to record
5.	更	adv	gèng		even more
6.	有人	p	yǒurén		some people
7.	簡單	adj	jiǎndān		simple
8.	複雜	adj	fǔzá		complicated
9.	簡化	v	jiǎnhuà		simplified, to simplify
10.	簡體	n	jiǎntǐ		simplified style
11.	筆畫	n	bǐhuà	(筆)	strokes
12.	比較	adj	bǐjiǎo		comparatively
13.	繁體	n	fántǐ		complicated style
14.	所有的	p	suǒyǒude		all
15.	鐘頭	n	zhōngtóu		hour
16.	雖然	conj	suīrán		although
17.	前頭	n	qiántou		front
18.	畫兒	n	huàr		picture
19.	認	v	rèn		to try to recognize
20.	可不是嗎?		kě bushì ma?		exactly!

Text (traditional characters)

高文和毛美文討論寫漢字。下邊兒是他們的談話：

高　你覺得學中文最大的困難是甚麼？

毛　是漢字。

高　你喜歡寫字嗎？

毛　喜歡。我最喜歡寫字了。但是漢字不容易記，也不容易寫。

高　有人告訴過我，現在漢字有兩種了：一種是簡單的，一種是複雜的，
　　對不對？

毛　對。一種是簡化的漢字，叫簡化字，筆畫比較少，也比較容易寫。一
　　種是舊漢字，叫繁體字，筆畫多，比較難寫。

高　是不是所有的漢字都簡化了呢？

毛　不，簡體字比繁體字少得多。

高　要是兩種都得會寫，寫字就更難了，是不是？

毛　可不是嗎？但是漢字很好看，所以我還是喜歡寫。

高　你喜歡寫簡體字還是繁體字呢？

毛　很難說。簡體字雖然容易寫，但是沒有繁體字那麼好看。繁體字筆畫
　　雖然複雜，但是比簡體字好看得多。

高　你們寫字，所有的字都得寫得一樣大嗎？

毛　對了。老師開始的時候就告訴我們了：所有的字都應該寫得一樣大。

高　你寫幾個字給我看看，好不好？

毛　好...你看，我寫了四個字，寫得不好，寫得不一樣大。第四個寫得太
　　大了，比前頭的三個大得多。

高　你寫得真好看，每個字都像一個畫兒。我以前只學過說話，沒有學過
　　認字寫字。以後我也要學學寫字了。

LESSON XXVI

New Words (traditional characters)

1.	日記	n	rìjì	diary
2.	毛衣	n	máoyī	sweater
3.	衣服	n	yīfu	garment
4.	淺	adv	qiǎn	light (in color, shade)
5.	綠	adj	lǜ	green
6.	黃	adj	huáng	yellow
7.	白	adj	bái	white
8.	深	adv	shēn	deep (in color, shade)
9.	藍	adj	lán	blue
10.	樣子	n	yàngzi	style, shape
11.	顏色	n	yánsè	color
12.	塊	m	kuài	piece
13.	點心	n	diǎnxin	refreshment, pastry
14.	愛	v	ài	to like, to love
15.	廁所	n	cèsuǒ	toilet
16.	腳步	n	jiǎobù	footstep
17.	聲音	n	shēngyin	noise, sound
18.	安靜	v-o	ānjìng	quiet
19.	搬家	v-o	bānjiā	to move one's residence
20.	同志	n	tóngzhì	comrade (a general title for men and women)
21.	錶	n	biǎo	watch
22.	也…也	conj	yě…yě	both…and

小謝的日記

一月十一號

到美國來了快五個月了。今天第一次一個人進城去買東西。街上的人很不少，但是沒有北京那麼多。

毛衣穿壞了，想去買一件新的，但是沒買成。雖然現在才一月，但是所有的地方都已經開始賣夏天的衣服了。毛衣很少，並且不是淺紅的，淺綠的，就是淺黃的，或者白的。我想買一件黑的，或者深藍的，但是他們說沒有。他們說聖誕節以前，樣子也多，顏色也多。

高文剛才來了，給我帶了來一塊點心。這個人別的都好，就是不喜歡學習，自己不愛看書，也不讓別人看書。

這間屋子在廁所旁邊，腳步的聲音真多。我想我還得搬一次家。下星期到老黃那兒去看看，他那兒好像很安靜。

友和*讓應**同志給我帶來了一個錶。錶很好。但是也讓我更想她們了。

*Yǒuhé: a given name
**Yīng: a surname

New Words (traditional characters)

1.	把	fv	bǎ	to take hold of
2.	糟糕	int	zāogāo	oh dear (what a mess)
3.	送	v	sòng	to give as a present
4.	圓珠筆	n	yuánzhūbǐ	ball-point pen
5.	丟	v	diū	to lose
6.	再	adv	zài	again, once more
7.	不好意思	adj	bùhǎoyìsi	embarrassing, embarrassed
8.	生產	v	shēngchǎn	to produce
9.	工廠	n	gōngchǎng	factory
10.	咳	int	hài	sound of regret or mild disgust
11.	停	v	tíng	to park (a car)
12.	自來水	n	zìláishuǐ	running water
13.	洗	v	xǐ	to wash
14.	百	nu	bǎi	hundred
15.	塊	m	kuài	dollar
16.	錢	n	qián	money
17.	講話	n	jiǎnghuà	lecture
18.	大意	n	dàyì	general idea
19.	怕	v	pà	to be afraid (of)
20.	哎呀	int	āiyā	oh dear
21.	教室	n	jiàoshǐ	classroom

Text (traditional characters)

I

謝新民　糟糕！我把小張送給我的圓珠筆丟了。
毛美文　你可以請他再給你一枝。
　謝　　不好意思吧？
　毛　　沒關係。他家有個生產圓珠筆的工廠。每年都生產得太多，所以
　　　　他和他哥哥都把太多的送給朋友。
　謝　　咳！我不知道，不好意思了半天！

II

　謝　　誰把車停在這兒了？
　高　　我。這是我的車。
　謝　　你爲甚麼把車開到這兒來？
　高　　因爲這兒有自來水。我想把車洗一洗。
　謝　　爲甚麼要洗車？
　高　　我要用錢，想把車賣了。沒賣以前，把它洗乾淨了，也許可以多
　　　　賣一百塊錢。

III

　毛　　今天上午我沒能去上課。你能不能把老師講話的大意告訴我？
　高　　他的講話很複雜。我怕記不住，所以把他說的話都記在本子上了。
　　　　你可以看看。
　毛　　好。你的本子呢？
　高　　在這兒...哎呀，糟糕，我把本子忘在教室裡了！

LESSON XXVIII

New Words (traditional characters)

1.	座	m	zuò	M for buildings or massive objects
2.	房子	n	fángzi	house
3.	大樓	n	dàlóu	tall building
4.	又...又		yòu...yòu	not only...but also
5.	亮	adj	liàng	bright
6.	房錢	n	fángqián	rent
7.	貴	adj	guì	expensive
8.	付	v	fù	to pay
9.	除了...以外		chúle...yǐwài	except, besides
10.	電費	n	diànfèi	electricity charge (fee)
11.	毛	m	máo	dime
12.	分	m	fēn	cent
13.	空氣	n	kōngqì	air
14.	缺點	n	quēdiǎn	drawback
15.	睡	v	shuì	to sleep
16.	起	v	qǐ	to get up
17.	關(上)	v	guān (shang)	to turn off
18.	附近	n	fùjìn	vicinity
19.	合適	adj	héshì	suitable, fitting
20.	服務員	n	fúwùyuán	attendant
21.	一共	adv	yīgòng	altogether
22.	找	v	zhǎo	to give change to

I

謝新民　老黃，我覺得你這座房子比我住的那個大樓好得多。你的屋子
　　　　又乾淨又亮，這兩個窗戶真大。

黃　　但是房錢貴啊！

謝　　你每〔個〕月付多少房錢？

黃　　一個月二百零五塊〔錢〕。

謝　　只比我多五塊錢，不到百分之三。

黃　　但是我除了房錢以外，還得付電費呢！

謝　　電費多少錢一個月？

黃　　電費兩個月付一次。每次二十二塊兩毛五分錢。

謝　　但是你的屋子很安靜，空氣也好。

黃　　除了有點兒貴以外，這個地方還有一個缺點。這兒住的人除了
　　　　我以外，都不是學生，都喜歡早睡早起。每天十一點以後，一定
　　　　要把收音機關上。

謝　　現在我才知道，你這兒不比我那兒好。在學校附近要找到合適的
　　　　房子真不容易。

服務員1　您要買甚麼？

　學生1　你們有圓珠筆嗎？

服務員2　有，都在這兒。我們有一塊錢一枝的，有五毛錢一枝的，也有兩毛五分錢一枝的。您要哪種？

　學生2　我試試。…這種五毛錢一枝的不錯。

服務員3　對了。又好看又便宜。

　學生3　好，我要一枝。那些英漢字典一本多少錢？

服務員4　九塊五一本。

　學生4　有沒有便宜一點兒的？

服務員5　這本小（一）點兒的比較便宜，六塊七毛五一本。

　學生5　好。我買一本綠的。一共多少錢？

服務員6　一共七塊兩毛五。…您給了十塊錢，我找您兩塊七毛五。

　學生6　好。再見。

服務員7　再見。

LESSON XXIX

New Words (traditional characters)

1.	表演	v	biǎoyǎn	to give a performance
2.	春假	n	chūnjià	spring vacation
3.	計劃	n	jìhua	plan
4.	查	v	chá	to look up (information)
5.	論文	n	lùnwén	thesis
6.	提前	adv	tíqián	ahead of schedule
7.	完成	v	wánchéng	to complete
8.	可惜	v	kěxī	too bad
9.	不然	conj	bùrán	otherwise
10.	紐約	n	Niǔyuē	New York City
11.	音樂	n	yīnyuè	music
12.	甚麼的	p	shénmede	and so forth
13.	旅行	v	lǚxíng	to travel
14.	批評	v	pīping	to criticize
15.	一天到晚	adv	yītiān dàowǎn	all day long, all the time
16.	睡覺	v-o	shuìjiào	to sleep
17.	不但...而且	conj	bùdàn...érqiě	not only...but also
18.	老	adv	lǎo	keep on (doing something)
19.	一邊(兒)...一邊(兒)	conj	yībiān(r)...yībiān(r)	V1 while V2
20.	大聲(兒)	adv	dàshēng(r)	loudly
21.	幹	v	gàn	to do (same as 作)

高文　小謝，去年你表演了一次唱歌兒。今年還表演嗎？

謝新民　今年不表演了。

高　我很喜歡聽唱歌兒。我真希望你再表演一次。

謝　我現在沒有時間搞這些了。

高　下星期放春假，你有甚麼計劃？想出去玩兒玩兒嗎？

謝　我不能出去，我得在圖書館裡查查書。我希望能把論文提前完成。

高　你不應該不休息啊！可惜我已經把車賣了。不然我一定帶你到紐約去玩兒玩兒，去聽聽音樂，吃吃中國飯，看看話劇，甚麼的。

謝　老黃買了新車。你可以找他一起去。

高　我不想再跟老黃一起旅行了。他太愛批評人。去年我跟他一起旅行的時候兒，他一天到晚批評我。不是說我開車開得太快，就是說我睡覺睡得太多。他自己呢？不但吃得很多，而且老一邊兒吃一邊兒大聲兒〔地〕說話。我不喜歡這種批評人的人。

謝　那麼你現在正在幹甚麼呢？

高　我...我...我...

LESSON XXX

New Words (traditional characters)

1.	早	adj	zǎo	good morning
2.	太太	n	tàitai	Mrs., wife
3.	先生	n	xiānsheng	Mr., husband
4.	流利	adj	liúlì	fluent
5.	最近	adv	zuìjìn	recently, recent
6.	又	adv	yòu	again
7.	下兒	m	xiàr	M for action
8.	關心	v	guānxīn	to be concerned about
9.	聽説	v	tīngshuō	to have heard people say
10.	一天比一天		yītiān bǐ yītiān	day by day
11.	提高	v	tígāo	to raise
12.	情況	n	qíngkuàng	condition
13.	算是	adv	suànshi	to be considered as
14.	進步	adj	jìnbù	improved, progressive
15.	許多	adj	xǔduō	many, lots of
16.	需要	v	xūyào	to need
17.	解決	v	jiějué	to solve
18.	國家	n	guójiā	country, nation
19.	恐怕	adv	kǒngpà	I am afraid that
20.	得很	int	--dehěn	extremely

謝新民　您早！白太太。

白太太　您早！謝先生。您是甚麼時候來美國的？

謝　我是半年前來的。您的中國話說得真流利。

白　哪裡哪裡！我以前去過中國。

謝　您是甚麼時候兒去的？

白　三十多年以前。在中國住過兩年。

謝　您最近又去過沒有？

白　沒有。回來〔了〕以後沒有再去過，但是我非常關心中國。聽說中國現在發展得很快。每個人都有飯吃，有衣服穿。生活水平也一天比一天提高了。

謝　現在的情況算是比從前進步了，但是生產上還有許多問題需要解決。

白　我希望能跟您多談談。下星期四您有沒有時間來參加一個晚會？我希望您能把您國家最近的情況給大家介紹一下兒。

謝　對不起。我最近有點兒忙。下星期要到紐約去兩天。恐怕沒時間參加晚會。對不起得很！

白　沒關係。我以後再請您。

LESSON XXXI

New Words (traditional characters)

1.	用不着	v	yòngbuzháo	unneeded, to have no need for
2.	放	v	fàng	to put
3.	安排	v	ānpái	to arrange
4.	夠	adj	gòu	enough
5.	最好	adv	zuìhǎo	it would be best
6.	重	adj	zhòng	heavy
7.	推	v	tuī	to push
8.	主意	n	zhúyi (zhǔyi)	idea
9.	牆	n	qiáng	wall
10.	掉	v	diào	to fall off
11.	難看	adj	nánkàn	ugly
12.	相片(兒)	n	xiàngpiān(r)	photograph
13.	掛	v	guà	to hang up
14.	糖	n	táng	sugar, candy
15.	水果	n	shuǐguǒ	fruit
16.	幫助	v	bāngzhù	to help
17.	錄音帶	n	lùyīndài	audiotape
18.	跑	v	pǎo	to run
19.	發音	n	fāyīn	pronunciation

晚會以前

小張　今天晚上的晚會有多少人參加？

毛美文　有五，六十人吧！我們應該把用不着的東西放回去，把桌子椅
　　　　子安排一下兒。椅子夠不夠？

張　　不夠。最好能把門外邊兒的那張大椅子搬進來。

毛　　我們可以試試。

張　　我想太重了，我們兩個人搬不進來。

毛　　再找一個人來一起搬。三個人就搬得進來了。

張　　再把這兩把小椅子搬過去，把門旁邊兒的大桌子推過來一點兒。

毛　　這個主意不錯。把大桌子推過來以後，大家走出去走進來就方便
　　　得多了。

張　　你看，牆上的那張畫兒快掉下來了。那張畫兒又舊又難看。

毛　　把它拿下來，把你屋子裡的那張大相片掛上去，怎麼樣？

張　　好。我們開始吧！

毛　　剛才買的糖和水果還在車裡呢！我去把那些東西拿進來。你去找
　　　一下兒史家明。請她幫助我們。

張　　她在哪兒呢？

毛　　我走下樓來的時候兒，她正拿着很多錄音帶跑上樓去。她一定在
　　　屋子裡練習發音呢！

LESSON XXXII

New Words (traditional characters)

1.	吸煙	v-o	xīyān		to smoke
2.	台	m	tái		measure word
3.	電視(機)	n	diànshì(jī)	（台）	television (set)
4.	修理	v	xiūli		to repair
5.	緊張	adj	jǐnzhāng		tense
6.	對	prep	duì		toward, to
7.	組織	v	zǔzhi		to organize
8.	克服	v	kèfú		to overcome
9.	工夫	n	gōngfu		free time
10.	好處	n	hǎochu		advantage
11.	自在	adj	zìzai		comfortable, at ease
12.	節目	n	jiému		program
13.	簡直	adv	jiǎnzhí		simply
14.	包	m, v	bāo		package, to wrap up
15.	茶	n	chá		tea
16.	喝	v	hē		to drink
17.	杯	m	bēi		cupful
18.	法國	n	Fàguó (Fǎguó)		France
19.	酒	n	jiǔ		wine, liquor
20.	又...了	adv	yòu...le		again(!)

謝新民　高文，你不是早就決定不吸煙了嗎？怎麼今天又吸起來了？

高文　我剛把這台電視機修理好，修理得太緊張了。現在想看看電視，吸吸煙，休息一下兒。

謝　看起來不吸煙很難，但是我覺得你應該想出一個辦法來。這樣吸下去，對身體不好。

高　這件事說起來容易，作起來難。

謝　不少人都有這個問題。也許你應該把這兒所有的吸煙的人都組織起來，大家互相幫助，克服你們的困難。

高　你想出來的辦法好是好，但是誰有工夫呢？並且，吸煙有時候兒也有好處。像今天吧，又刮風，又下雨。也不能散步，也不能打球。（要是）不吸煙能幹甚麼呢？

謝　看電視還不夠自在嗎？

高　這些節目很沒有意思。吸着煙看，還看得下去，不吸煙，簡直看不下去。

謝　我想起來了：我上星期買了一包綠茶，我請你喝一杯中國茶。

高　謝謝你。要是你有法國酒就更好了！

LESSON XXXIII

New Words (traditional characters)

1.	早上	n	zǎoshang	morning
2.	雨衣	n	yǔyī	raincoat
3.	小心	adj	xiǎoxīn	careful
4.	早飯	n	zǎofàn	breakfast
5.	百貨大樓	n	bǎihuòdàlóu	department store
6.	一塊兒	adv	yīkuàr	together
7.	最後	adv	zuìhòu	finally
8.	午飯	n	wǔfàn	lunch
9.	各	sp	gè	each, various
10.	躺	v	tǎng	to lie down
11.	牀	n	chuáng	bed
12.	預告	n	yùgào	forecast
13.	笑	v	xiào	to laugh, to smile
14.	記得	v	jìde	to remember
15.	提	v	tí	to mention
16.	機會	n	jīhuì	chance, opportunity
17.	小時	n	xiǎoshí	hour

高文進城

　　春天到了，差不多天天下雨，街上人人都穿着雨衣。高文去年不小〔心〕把雨衣丟了。今天早上，他決定再買一件。吃完了早飯就進城去了。

　　快到百貨大樓的時候兒，高文遇見了一個從前的同屋。他也是去買〔雨〕衣的。他們就説着話一塊兒走進了百貨大樓，找到賣雨衣的地方。雨衣的樣子真不少，件件都很漂亮。他們看了半天，試了好幾件，最後每人買〔了〕一件，在一起吃了午飯，就各人回到各人的學校去了。

　　高文走進（他）屋子的時候兒，他同屋正躺在牀上聽天氣預告呢！〔一〕看見高文，他就説："明天又要下雨了。"高文説："沒關係，我雨衣已經買來了。"説完，就把雨衣拿出來給他同屋看。他同屋一看就笑起來了。他説："我也買了一件完完全全一樣的。"高文問他："你用了多少錢？"他同屋説："我用了五十九塊九毛五。你呢？"高文説："我不告訴你。"他同屋説："我看出來了：我買得比你便宜，是不是？"

　　高文説："對了。我知道我不應該在城裡買東西。我記得你以前提過合作社裡的東西比較便宜。但是今天早上我不想念書，想找個機會到城裡去看看，看看城裡有沒有新東西賣，所以很早就進城去了。"

　　"那麼城裡有沒有新東西賣呢？"他的同屋問。

　　"我沒注意。我遇見了一個朋友，跟他説了一個多小時的話，忘了注意這件事了。"

New Words (traditional characters)

1.	...室	suf	...shǐ	(a) room for...
2.	近代	n	jìndài	modern period
3.	思想	n	sīxiǎng	thoughts
4.	瑪立	n	Mǎlì	woman's name -- Mary
5.	研究	v	yánjiu	to do research in
6.	五四	n	wǔsì	May Fourth
7.	運動	n	yùndòng	movement
8.	題目	n	tímu	topic
9.	越...越	conj	yuè...yuè	the more...the more
10.	生日	n	shēngrì	birthday
11.	禮物	n	lǐwu	gift
12.	唱片(兒)	n	chàngpiān(r)	record
13.	文化	n	wénhuà	culture
14.	民間	n	mínjiān	folk, popular (among people)
15.	故事	n	gùshi	story
16.	語言	n	yǔyán	language
17.	學院	n	xuéyuàn	institute
18.	爲	fv	wèi	for the sake of, in order to
19.	年輕	adj	niánqīng	young
20.	歲	n	suì	years of age
21.	頭髮	n	tóufa	hair

在學生休息室裡

I

謝新民　《中國近代思想史》。這本書是誰的?
高文　是瑪立的。她最近研究起五四運動來了。她說這個題目越研究越有意思。今年夏天還要研究下去呢!
謝　瑪立這會兒是不是不在這兒?
高　她去打電話〔去〕了。你要找她嗎? 她一會兒就回來。
謝　不。我找你。送給她的生日禮物,你想出來了沒有?
高　我已經買了。我買了一張唱片兒——一張新出來的唱片兒。我希望她喜歡。你買了甚麼?
謝　我還沒想出來呢! 我越想越拿不定主意。你替我想想。
高　她喜歡中國文化。你可以給她買一本中國民間故事書。
謝　你想得真好。這個主意不錯。我一會兒就去買。

II

謝　毛美文,聽說你要到北京語言學院去工作了。我真為你高興。
毛　我非常高興。可惜北京我沒有朋友。
謝　我大哥家在語言學院附近。到了北京,你可以去找找他。
毛　那好極了。你大哥像你一樣嗎?
謝　他很喜歡朋友,特別是年輕的朋友。
毛　你大哥今年多大?
謝　他比我大五歲,快四十歲了。
毛　你已經三十多了嗎? 我沒有看出來。你看上去和我們一樣大。
謝　不,我比你們大得多。你看,我已經有白頭髮了。

LESSON XXXV

New Words (traditional characters)

1.	夜裡	n	yèli	in the night
2.	連...也/都		lián...yě/dōu	even...
3.	對不住	v	duìbuzhù	to be sorry (to be unable to face someone)
4.	害	v	hài	to cause
5.	一直	adv	yīzhí	continuously, all along
6.	中學	n	zhōngxué	high school
7.	西方	n	xīfāng	western
8.	從來	adv	cónglái	all along
9.	千	nu	qiān	thousand
10.	專業	n	zhuānyè	field of concentration
11.	歷史	n	lìshǐ	history
12.	方面	n	fāngmiàn	respect, aspect
13.	請教	v	qǐngjiào	to ask for instruction or advice
14.	選	v	xuǎn	to elect
15.	門	m	mén	M for academic courses
16.	文學	n	wénxué	literature
17.	如果	conj	rúguǒ	if
18.	解釋	v	jiěshì	explain
19.	只要...就	conj	zhǐyào...jiù	so long as, if only

瑪立　小謝，你給我的那本書，我越看越放不下。昨天夜裡看了半本，連覺都差不多沒睡。

謝　　太對不住了，害你沒睡覺。你真那麼喜歡那些故事嗎？

瑪　　非常喜歡。我一直很愛看民間故事。在中學的時候兒，只要有工夫，我就到圖書館去看民間故事的書。連最簡單的我也看，所以西方的故事看了不少，但是從來沒看過東方的民間故事。中國有四千多年的文化，民間故事一定很多。

謝　　這兒的圖書館裡這種書多得很。

瑪　　好極了。我的專業是中國歷史，所以應該多看一些這方面的書。中國歷史有些地方我不太清楚，以後可以請教你嗎？

謝　　別說請教。只要我知道，我一定告訴你。我這學期選了一門美國文學史，以後在英文方面如果有問題，也要請你解釋解釋呢！

瑪　　好，我們互相幫助，互相學習吧！

LESSON XXXVI

New Words (traditional characters)

1.	問路	v	wènlù	to ask for directions
2.	請問	v	qǐngwèn	Please, may I ask...
3.	火車	n	huǒchē	train
4.	站	suf	zhàn	station
5.	離	pre	lí	from
6.	遠	adj	yuǎn	far
7.	路	n	lù	road, route (no.__)
8.	多	adv	duō (duó)	how
9.	近	adj	jìn	near
10.	往	fv	wàng	toward
11.	街口兒	n	jiēkǒur	intersection (of streets)
12.	轉	v	zhuǎn	turn
13.	條	m	tiáo	M for streets
14.	郵局	n	yóujú	post office
15.	公園(兒)	n	gōngyuán(r)	park
16.	花兒	n	huār	flowers
17.	校園(兒)	n	xiàoyuán(r)	schoolyard
18.	經過	v	jīngguò	to pass by
19.	迎春	n	yíngchūn	forsythia
20.	大概	adv	dàgài	probably
21.	感到	v	gǎndao	to feel
22.	永遠	adv	yǒngyuǎn	forever
23.	有詩意	adj	yǒushīyì	poetic

I

問路

A 1　　請問，去火車站怎麼走？
B 1　　火車站離這兒很遠，最好坐二十二路公共汽車去。
A 2　　公共汽車站離這兒有多遠？
B 2　　公共汽車站離這兒比較近。從這兒往前走，走到前頭的街口兒，
　　　　往左轉，再往前走，過了兩條街，你就會看見個郵局。過了郵局，
　　　　你就可以看見個公園兒。公共汽車站就在公園兒的前邊兒。
A 3　　謝謝！謝謝！

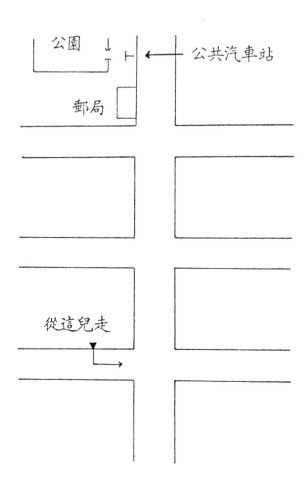

II

看花兒

高文　今天天氣多麼暖和啊！我們到校園兒裡去散散步吧！

史家明　好吧！昨天經過大圖書館的時候兒，看見很多迎春花兒已經黃了，今天這麼暖和，大概已經開開了吧！

高　我們去看看吧！你喜歡迎春嗎？

史　喜歡，你呢？

高　我也很喜歡。很多人都喜歡這種花兒。我想這是因為迎春開得最早。大家經過了一個很長的冬天以後，看見了一些黃黃的花兒，都感到特別高興。

史　我想迎春這個名字很好。"迎"是歡迎的意思，"春"當然是春天。"歡迎春天"，多（麼）有意思啊！別的花兒的名字，我常常記不住，但是迎春這個名字我永遠忘不了。這個名字多麼有詩意啊！

LESSON XXXVII

New Words (traditional characters)

1.	週末	n	zhōumò	weekend
2.	華盛頓	n	Huáshèngdùn	Washington
3.	參觀	v	cānguān	to visit (a place)
4.	各處	n	gèchù	various places
5.	戲	n	xì	play
6.	滿意	v	mǎnyì	to be satisfied
7.	本來	adv	běnlái	originally
8.	音樂會	n	yīnyuèhuì	concert
9.	座位	n	zuòwei	seat
10.	讓	fv	ràng	by
11.	只好	adv	zhǐhǎo	have no choice but to
12.	演員	n	yǎnyuán	actor, actress
13.	第一流	adj	dìyīliú	first-rate
14.	被	fv	bèi	by
15.	海	n	hǎi	sea
16.	英里	m	yīnglǐ	mile
17.	游泳	v	yóuyǒng	to swim
18.	樣兒	n	yàngr	style
19.	杯子	n	bēizi	cup, glass
20.	襯衫	n	chènshān	shirt, blouse
21.	累	adj	lèi	tired
22.	以為	v	yǐwéi	to think wrongly (thought)
23.	可是	conj	kěshì	but

瑪立　小謝，你週末玩兒了還是念書了？

謝新民　玩兒了。前天從華盛頓來了一個老同學。他要參觀我們的大學。我帶他到各處去走了走。昨天下午看了一個戲。

瑪　　〔戲〕看得怎麼樣？

謝　　看得一點兒也不滿意。我本來是想帶他去聽音樂會的，但是決定得太晚，好的座位都讓人買去了，所以只好去看戲。他們說那些演員都是第一流的，但是我覺得他們演得一點兒也不好。你幹了甚麼了？

瑪　　我被一個朋友請去，在海邊兒上玩兒了一天。

謝　　這時候兒去海邊兒，不冷嗎？

瑪　　我也以為會冷。沒想到一點兒也不冷。我們是騎車去的，騎了二十多英里，騎得有一點兒熱。

謝　　你們游泳了沒有？

瑪　　沒有。我們只散散步，在各處看看。我朋友的哥哥在離海邊兒不遠的地方開了一個店。我們到那個店裡去買了一些東西。他們的東西賣得真便宜。你看，這樣兒的杯子才兩塊五毛錢一個。

謝　　你穿着的襯衫很漂亮，也是在那兒買的嗎？

瑪　　對了。才九塊錢一件。多便宜！

謝　　聽上去你週末過得很好。

瑪　　可是我昨天騎車騎得太多了。今天覺得很累。一點兒也不想工作，老想睡覺。

LESSON XXXVIII

New Words (traditional characters)

1.	畢業	v, n	bìyè	to graduate, graduation
2.	典禮	n	diǎnlǐ	ceremony
3.	舉行	v	jǔxíng	to hold a ceremony
4.	萬	nu, n	wàn	ten thousand, a surname
5.	祖父	n	zǔfù	grandfather
6.	旅館	n	lǚguǎn	hotel
7.	滿	adj	mǎn	full
8.	愛人	n	àiren	husband, wife
9.	定	v	dìng	to reserve
10.	房間	n	fángjiān	room
11.	校友	n	xiàoyǒu	alumnus/a
12.	造船	v-o	zàochuán	to make ships, ship building
13.	公司	n	gōngsī	company
14.	等…再	adv	děng…zài	wait until
15.	結果	adv	jiéguǒ	as a result
16.	照相	v-o	zhàoxiàng	to take pictures
17.	票(子)	n	piào(zi)	ticket
18.	上海	n	Shànghǎi	Shanghai
19.	代表	v	dàibiǎo	to represent
20.	飽	adj	bǎo	full (from eating)

Text (traditional characters)

高文　這兩天校園裡人真多。大概校友們都回來參加畢業典禮了。

張力　畢業典禮哪天舉行？

高　　星期四，就是後天。我的同屋萬大爲今年畢業。他家裡的人昨天就已經來了。連他（的）八十多歲的祖父也來了。

張　　哦，所以各處的旅館都住得那麼滿！上星期我要替我弟弟和他的愛人定一個房間，打了很多電話，怎麼定也定不着。所有的旅館都說，"一個房間也沒有了，連最貴的房間也被人定去了。"

高　　你弟弟他們也要來參加畢業典禮嗎？

張　　不，他們要來參觀一家造船公司的，現在他們決定等下個月再來了。

高　　你去不去看畢業典禮呢？

張　　我不去。你想去嗎？

高　　我一定得去。張友文給了我一張票子。他家裡的人都在上海，當然不能來看他畢業了。

張　　你應該去，你可以代表他家裡的人。但是最好早早兒地去。有一年，老黃的女朋友畢業，老黃去了。典禮九點才開始，雖然他八點半就到了校園，可是已經連一個座位也沒有了。他說人真多，他怎麼找也找不着座位。最後是站在大圖書館前邊看的。結果，甚麼也看不清楚，連相都沒照成。所以，你得早早兒地去，別像老黃那年一樣。

LESSON XXXIX

New Words (traditional characters)

1.	好久不見		hǎojiǔbujiàn	Haven't seen you for a long time
2.	見面	v-o	jiànmiàn	to see each other
3.	呀	int	yā	interjection particle
4.	生病	v-o	shēngbìng	to be sick
5.	飛機	n	fēijī	airplane
6.	中國民航	n	Zhōngguómínháng	CAAC (Chinese airline)
7.	東京	n	Dōngjīng	Tokyo
8.	先...再	adv	xiān...zài	first...then
9.	飛機場	n	fēijīchǎng	airport
10.	等	v	děng	to wait
11.	糊塗	adj	hútu	muddle-headed
12.	上	v	shàng	to board (a vehicle)
13.	公路	n	gōnglù	highway
14.	定	v	dìng	to set, settled
15.	號	n	hào	number (ordinal)
16.	班機	n	bānjī	flight
17.	通	v	tōng	to communicate by letter, telephone, etc.
18.	啦	par	la	rhetorical particle
19.	見	v	jiàn	to see
20.	幫忙	v-o	bāngmáng	to help

Text (traditional characters)

喂，喂，…我就是。你是老黃吧！…我一聽就聽出來是你。好久
不見！我們有兩個月沒有見面了吧？…我呀？我這幾天哪兒也沒去。
我的車讓弟弟給借去了，今天才還我的。你怎麼樣？…甚麼？你要回
台北去？…　哦！你母親生甚麼病？…哦。你甚麼時候走？…坐哪家
公司的飛機？…坐中國民航的飛機？中國民航的飛機到得了台北嗎？
…哦，你先到東京，再坐日航…èi，這個主意不錯。…你在東京飛機場
要等多少時候呢？…要等四個半鐘頭？太長了！你在東京有朋友嗎？
…哦，大爲在東京，我忘了。你看我多（麼）糊塗！…你明天晚上就
走？有人送你上飛機場嗎？…我送你去飛機場，怎麼樣？…沒關係，
你不用去找別人了。…不，不，那是去年的事。我現在已經不怕開公
路了，現在哪兒都能去了。…好，說定了。我明天一定送你。…你要
我幾點去我就幾點去，甚麼時候都行。…可以，可以。…沒關係，我
明天一定五點鐘到你那兒。…好，好。（你）有甚麼別的事我可以幫
忙嗎？…大爲知道你坐幾號班機嗎？…哦，你們已經通過電話啦？好
極了。…好，好。明天見…明天見！

LESSON XL

New Words (traditional characters)

1.	留學	v	liúxué	to study abroad
2.	封	m	fēng	M for letter
3.	親愛	adj	qīn'ài	dear
4.	時差	n	shíchā	time difference
5.	離開	v	líkai	to leave
6.	高	adj	gāo	tall
7.	對於	prep	duìyú	to, in
8.	興趣	n	xìngqù	interest
9.	醒	v	xǐng	to wake up
10.	下	v	xià	to get off, dismount
11.	將來	adv	jiānglái	in the future
12.	印象	n	yìnxiàng	impression
13.	深	adj	shēn	deep
14.	青年	n	qīngnián	youth
15.	自由	adj	zìyóu	freedom
16.	活潑	adj	huópò	lively
17.	友誼	n	yǒuyí	friendship
18.	不斷地	adv	bùduànde	unceasingly
19.	增長	v	zēngzhǎng	to grow
20.	交流	n	jiāoliú	exchange
21.	起...作用	v	qǐ...zuòyòng	to produce...effect
22.	單元	n	dānyuán	apartment

23.	廚房	n	chúfáng	kitchen
24.	衛生間	n	wèishēngjiān	bathroom
				(hygiene room)
25.	熱烈	adv	rèliè	heartily
26.	快樂	adj	kuàilè	happy
27.	女兒	n	nǚ'er	daughter

謝新民在美國留學了一年，上個月回國去了。下邊兒是他回國以後寫來的第一封信：

親愛的同學們，

我到家已經快一個月了，大概因為時差吧：我一直覺得很累，老覺得睡不夠，所以今天才給你們寫信。對不起得很！

中國和一年前差不多，但是我的女兒比我離開的時候高得多了。她對於你們給她的小火車特別有興趣，天天一醒就下牀去找她的火車。她說她將來要坐火車到美國去呢！

過去一年裡，我認為給我印象最深的是美國青年了。你們不但思想自由，活潑，而且對朋友也非常熱情。你們給我的幫助是我永遠忘不了的。我希望我們的友誼能不斷地增長，能在中美兩國（的）文化交流上起一些作用。

下月我們要搬家了，要搬進一個大一點兒的單元去。除了廚房，衛生間以外，還有三間大屋子。瑪立來了以後，一定要在我們家住幾天。我和我愛人都熱烈地歡迎你來住。

我愛人要謝謝你們。你們送給她的那本書，對於她的工作非常有用。

今天我就寫這些了，別的下次再寫。希望我們能常常通信。

　　　祝你們

快樂！

　　　　　　　　　　　　　　　小謝
　　　　　　　　　　　　　　　六月十二號

Simplified Characters

LESSON I

New Words (simplified characters)

1.	学生	n	xuésheng	student
2.	老师	n	lǎoshī	teacher
3.	您	p	nín	you (polite form)
4.	是	v	shì	to be
5.	美国	n	Měiguó	U.S.A.
6.	人	n	rén	person
7.	吗	par	ma	question particle
8.	我	p	wǒ	I, me
9.	不	adv	bù	not, no
10.	中国	n	Zhōngguó	China
11.	你	p	nǐ	you
12.	这	sp	zhè, zhèi	this
13.	书	n	shū	book
14.	那	sp	nà, nèi	that
15.	报	n	bào	newspaper
16.	他	p	tā	he

Text (simplified characters)

I

学生	老师，您是美国人吗？
老师	我不是美国人，我是中国人。你是美国人吗？
学生	我是美国人。

II

学生	这是中国书吗？
老师	这是中国书。
学生	那是中国书吗？
老师	那不是中国书，那是中国报。

III

老师	他是学生吗？
学生	他是学生。
老师	他是中国学生吗？
学生	他不是中国学生，他是美国学生。

LESSON II

New Words (simplified characters)

1.	有	v	yǒu		to have
2.	一	nu	yī		one
3.	张	m	zhāng		measure word
4.	纸	n	zhǐ	（张）*	paper
5.	两	nu	liǎng		two
6.	很	adv	hěn		very
7.	大	adj	dà		big
8.	小	adj	xiǎo		small
9.	沒有	v	méiyou		to have not, to be without
10.	本	m	běn		measure word
11.	旧	adj	jiù		old
12.	新	adj	xīn		new
13.	好	adj	hǎo		good
14.	多	adj	duō		many
15.	老	adj	lǎo		old
16.	少	adj	shǎo		few
17.	三	nu	sān		three
18.	个	m	ge		measure word
19.	北京	n	Běijīng		Beijing (Peking)

---

*Words in parentheses in this column are the measure words most often associated with the preceding nouns

I

学生1	我有一张纸。你有纸吗？
学生2	我有纸。我有两张纸。
学生1	那两张纸大吗？
学生2	这两张纸不大，这两张纸很小。
学生1	你有中国报吗？
学生2	我没有中国报。

II

学生1	这两本书是旧书吗？
学生2	那两本书不是旧书，是新书。
学生1	新书好吗？
学生2	新书不好，旧书好。很多旧书很好。
学生1	这两本新书很大。
学生2	那两本新书不大，这本旧书大。

III

老师1	新学生多吗？
老师2	新学生不多。老学生多，新学生少。
老师1	那三个新学生是北京人吗？
老师2	不是北京人。很少学生是北京人。

LESSON III

New Words (simplified characters)

1.	毛笔	n	máobǐ	（枝）		writing brush
2.	钢笔	n	gāngbǐ	（枝）		fountain pen
3.	枝	m	zhī			measure word
4.	的	par	de			subordinating particle
5.	铅笔	n	qiānbǐ	（枝）		pencil
6.	长	adj	cháng			long
7.	短	adj	duǎn			short
8.	们	suf	-men			plural pronoun suffix
9.	黑板	n	hēibǎn	（个）		blackboard
10.	干净	adj	gānjing			clean
11.	本子	n	běnzi	（个，本）		notebook
12.	对不对		duìbudui			is it right?
13.	对了	v	duìle			(it is) right
14.	朋友	n	péngyou*			friend
15.	英国	n	Yīngguó			England
16.	英文	n	Yīngwén			English language
17.	中文	n	Zhōngwén			Chinese language

---

*Where no particular measure word is given, students may assume 个 (ge) is to be used.

I

学生1   你有沒有毛笔？

学生2   沒有，我没有毛笔。我有钢笔，我有一枝很新的钢笔。

学生1   你有沒有铅笔？

学生2   有，我有三枝长的，两枝短的。

学生1   你的那两枝短铅笔好不好？

学生2   不好，长铅笔好，短铅笔不好。

学生1   那本新书的纸好不好？

学生2   不好，很不好。

II

学生1   他们的黑板是新的，对不对？

学生2   对了，是新的。他们的那个大黑板很新。

学生1   那个新黑板干净不干净？

学生2   干净，他们的那个新黑板很干净。

学生1   你们的那个本子是不是新的？

学生2   不是，是旧的。

学生1   你们没〔有〕新本子，对不对？

学生2   不，我们有新本子，我们有很多新本子。

III

张老师有很多好朋友，他们是英国人，他们有很多英文书，英文报。张老师是中国人，他有中文报，没有英文报。

LESSON IV

New Words (simplified characters)

1.	工作	v	gōngzuò	to work
2.	只	adv	zhǐ	only
3.	学习	v	xuéxí	to study, learn
4.	看	v	kàn	to read, look at
5.	吗	int	ḿ	what (did you say)?
6.	呢	p	ne	question particle
7.	也	adv	yě	too, also
8.	几	nu	jǐ	how many, a few
9.	二	nu	èr	two
10.	四	nu	sì	four
11.	五	nu	wǔ	five
12.	六	nu	liù	six
13.	教	v	jiāo	to teach
14.	多少	nu	duōshao	how many
15.	十	nu	shí	ten
16.	七	nu	qī	seven
17.	八	nu	bā	eight
18.	九	nu	jiǔ	nine
19.	给	v	gěi	to give
20.	谢谢	v	xièxie	thank you

Text (simplified characters)

I

学生1	你工作不工作？
学生2	不工作。我只学习，我学习中文。
学生1	你看不看中文报？
学生2	嗨？
学生1	你看中文报不看？
学生2	不看。
学生1	你朋友呢？
学生2	他也不看。我们只看中文书。
学生1	你们有几本中文书？
学生2	有…一本，两本，三本，四本，五本，六本…有六本。
学生1	几本新的？几本旧的？
学生2	两本新的，四本旧的。

II

学生1	张老师教你不教？
学生2	教，他教我中文。他是（一）个很好的老师。
学生1	他只教中国学生吗？
学生2	不，他也教美国人。
学生1	他教多少学生？
学生2	他教三十七个学生。
学生1	他教多少美国学生？多少中国学生？
学生2	他教二十八个美国学生，九个中国学生。
学生1	你们（的）老师给你们本子不给？
学生2	不给。我们有本子，一个人有一个本子。

III

朋友1	你好吗？
朋友2	好，我很好。谢谢。你呢？
朋友1	我也很好，谢谢。

LESSON V

New Words (simplified characters)

1.	把	m	bǎ	measure word
2.	椅子	n	yǐzi	chair
3.	和	conj	hé	and
4.	桌子	n	zhuōzi	table, desk
5.	都	adv	dōu	all
6.	些	m	xiē	a few, some
7.	学校	n	xuéxiào	school
8.	人民	n	rénmín	people
9.	日报	n	rìbào	daily (newspaper)
10.	画报	n	huàbào	pictorial
11.	有意思	adj	yǒuyìsi	interesting
12.	学	v	xué	to learn (a skill), to study (a subject)
13.	日语	n	Rìyǔ	Japanese language
14.	还是	conj	háishi	--- or ---
15.	汉语	n	Hànyǔ	Chinese language
16.	会	v	huì	to know how, to be skillful in...
17.	作	v	zuò	to do (exercise), to make
18.	练习	n, v	liànxí	exercise, to practice
19.	用	v	yòng	to use

Text (simplified characters)

I

朋友1　　那两把椅子和那张桌子都是你的吗？
朋友2　　不。这些都不是我的，都是学校的。
朋友1　　你没有桌子和椅子吗？
朋友2　　没有。桌子和椅子我都没有。
朋友1　　那些人民日报和人民画报呢？也都是学校的吗？
朋友2　　不都是。这些人民画报是我的。
朋友1　　人民画报有意思还是人民日报有意思？
朋友2　　人民画报有意思。

II

中国朋友　　你学日语还是学汉语？
美国朋友　　我都学。我学一些日语，也学一些汉语。
中国朋友　　毛美文呢？他也都学吗？
美国朋友　　不，他只学日语，不学汉语，他会汉语。
中国朋友　　你们作练习不作？
美国朋友　　作，我们作很多练习。
中国朋友　　你们用钢笔（还是）用铅笔？
美国朋友　　铅笔，钢笔我们都用。

LESSON VI

New Words (simplified characters)

1.	贵姓		guìxìng	(What's your) honorable surname?
2.	姓	v, n	xìng	to have the surname of..., surname
3.	叫	v	jiào	to be called, to call
4.	什么	p	shénme	what ?
5.	名字	n	míngzi	name (full or first)
6.	怎么	adv	zěnme	how? why ?
7.	以前	adv	yǐqián	formerly
8.	怎么样		zěnmeyàng	how about...?
9.	吧	par	ba	suggestion particle
10.	位	m	wèi	M for people
11.	知道	v	zhīdao	to know (about a fact)
12.	山本	n	Shānběn	Yamamoto (Japanese surname)
13.	哪	sp	nǎ/něi	which?
14.	第	pref	dì	ordinal prefix
15.	日本	n	Rìběn	Japan
16.	谁	p	shéi	who?
17.	跟	conj	gēn	and
18.	同屋	n	tóngwū	roommate
19.	懂	v	dǒng	understand
20.	大学	n	dàxué	university, college

Text (simplified characters)

I

毛美文　您贵姓？

谢新民　我姓谢，我叫谢新民。你叫什么名字？

毛　我叫毛美文。我的英文名字叫Marion Mudd。中国朋友都叫我毛
　　　美文。

谢　你怎么有中文名字？

毛　我以前学习汉语，我们的老师给我们中文名字。

谢　你（的）这个名字很好。我也叫你毛美文，怎么样？

毛　好。我叫你什么呢？

谢　朋友都叫我小谢，你也叫我小谢吧！

II

谢　那三位老师都姓什么？你知道不知道？

毛　我知道。一个姓张，一个姓毛，一个姓山本。

谢　哪位姓张？

毛　第一位姓张。

谢　第二位呢？

毛　第二位姓毛。

谢　山本老师是日本人吧？

毛　对了，他是日本人，他教日语。

谢　他教谁日语？

毛　他教新学生日语。

谢　谁教你跟你同屋呢？

毛　张老师教我们。

谢　你的日语怎么样？

毛　不很好，懂一些。

谢　这个大学的学生都学习日语吗？

毛　不，不都学；很多人学汉语。

LESSON VII

New Words (simplified characters)

1.	年	n	nián	year
2.	忙	adj	máng	busy
3.	月	n	yuè	month
4.	今年	n	jīnnián	this year
5.	去	v	qù	to go
6.	今天	n	jīntiān	today
7.	来	v	lái	to come
8.	星期	n	xīngqī	week
9.	日	n	rì	day
10.	点(钟)	m	diǎn (zhōng)	o'clock (point on the clock)
11.	过	v	guò	to pass (time)
12.	刻	m	kè	quarter (of an hour)
13.	现在	n	xiànzài	now
14.	时候(儿)	n	shíhou(r)	time
15.	差	v	chà	to be short of
16.	分	n	fēn	minute
17.	半	m	bàn	half
18.	号	n	hào	ordinal day of month
19.	天	n	tiān	day
20.	零	nu	líng	zero

Text (simplified characters)

I

谢新民　你一年都很忙，对不对？

毛美文　不。我七月，八月，九月都不忙。

谢　今年你去不去中国？

毛　今年不去。

谢　你哪年去？

毛　我一九＿＿*年六月去。

II

毛　你朋友今天来不来？

谢　今天（是）星期几？

毛　星期三。

谢　今天他来。他星期一，（星期）三，（星期）五都来。

毛　星期日呢？

谢　星期日他不来。

毛　他几点钟来？

谢　他九点过一刻来。现在（是）什么时候儿？

毛　现在九点差五分。

III

朋友1　这些都是哪年的报？

朋友2　一些是这半年的，一些是一九八二年的。

朋友1　你有没有今年四月三号跟六号的报？

朋友2　没有，我没有那两天的报。

---

*Speaker may supply any number to make this a future year.

LESSON VIII

New Words (simplified characters)

1.	上午	n	shàngwǔ	morning
2.	到	fv	dào	(to go) to (a place)
3.	哪儿(哪里)p		nǎr (nǎli)	where
4.	那儿(那里)p		nàr (nàli)	there
5.	在	v	zài	to be at a place
6.	宿舍	n	sùshè	dormitory
7.	一起	adv	yīqǐ	together
8.	喜欢	v	xǐhuan	to like
9.	电影(儿)	n	diànyǐng(r)	movie
10.	下午	n	xiàwǔ	afternoon
11.	要	v	yào	to want to
12.	但是	conj	dànshi	but
13.	跟	fv	gēn	with
14.	从	fv	cóng	from
15.	这儿(这里)p		zhèr (zhèli)	here
16.	有事儿	adj	yǒushèr	not free, busy
17.	为什么	adv	wèishénme	why
18.	问	v	wèn	to ask (a question)
19.	前天	n	qiántiān	day before yesterday

Text (simplified characters)

I

小张　你上午到哪儿去？
毛美文　我到我朋友那儿去。
　张　你朋友在哪儿？
　毛　在宿舍。
　张　我上午也去宿舍。我们一起去，好吗？
　毛　好。

II

小张　你喜欢看电影吗？
毛美文　喜欢，很喜欢。
　张　你看不看今天下午的日本电影？
　毛　要看，但是不知道怎么去。
　张　我知道。你跟我去。两点半从我这儿去，怎么样？
　毛　两点半我在小谢那儿。我们从小谢那儿去，好不好？
　张　小谢也跟我们一起去吗？
　毛　不，他不去，他三点半有事儿。你为什么问？
　张　他不去看电影儿，你为什么要从他那儿去呢？
　毛　我要看前天的那张中文报。那张报在他那儿。我一点钟要到他那儿去。
　张　好。我两点半到小谢那儿去。

LESSON IX

New Words (simplified characters)

1.	外边(儿)	n	wàibian(r)	outside
2.	好看	adj	hǎokàn	good-looking
3.	里边(儿)	n	lǐbian(r)	inside
4.	舒服	adj	shūfu	comfortable
5.	自学	v	zìxué	to self-study, to do homework
6.	图书馆	n	túshūguǎn	library
7.	常常*	adv	chángcháng	frequently, most of the time
8.	杂志	n	zázhì	magazine
9.	地方	n	dìfang	place
10.	前边(儿)	n	qiánbian(r)	front
11.	后边(儿)	n	hòubian(r)	back
12.	左边(儿)	n	zuǒbian(r)	left side
13.	右边(儿)	n	yòubian(r)	right side
14.	上边(儿)	n	shàngbian(r)	top, above
15.	旁边(儿)	n	pángbian(r)	side
16.	下边(儿)	n	xiàbian(r)	bottom, below
17.	中间(儿)	n	zhōngjiàn(r)	middle, between, among
18.	有时候(儿)	adv	yǒushíhou(r)	sometimes
19.	她	p	tā	she, her

---

*may be shortened to 常 (cháng).

Text (simplified characters)

I

毛美文　我的宿舍很好。外边儿很好看。里边儿很干净，很舒服。

小谢　你常常在宿舍（里）自学吗？

毛　不。我常在图书馆（里）自学。那儿书多，杂志也多。

谢　你们的图书馆在什么地方？

毛　大的在宿舍前边儿，小的在宿舍后边儿。

谢　你去哪个？

毛　我常去宿舍后边儿的那个。

II

谢　哪张桌子是你的？

毛　左边儿的那张。右边儿的那张是我同屋的。

谢　你的桌子上有很多书。为什么她的桌子上沒有书？

毛　她不喜欢桌子上边儿有书。你看，她的书在椅子下边儿，椅子旁
边儿。

谢　你们的两张桌子中间儿也有很多书。那些书是谁的？

毛　也是她的。我的书都在桌子上。

III

谢　一年有十二个月，半年有六个月。

毛　对了，半年有六个月。

谢　一个月有三十一天。

毛　不对，不对！有时候只有三十天。二月常常只有二十八天。

谢　今年的二月有多少天？

毛　有二十九天。

LESSON X

New Words (simplified characters)

1.	念书	v-o	niànshū	to study
2.	得	par	de	verb particle
3.	高兴	adj	gāoxìng	cheerful, glad
4.	特别	adj, adv	tèbié	special, unusually
5.	看书	v-o	kànshū	to read (silently)
6.	写字	v-o	xiězì	to write
7.	快	adj	kuài	fast
8.	慢	adj	màn	slow
9.	说话	v-o	shuōhuà	to speak, to talk
10.	太	adv	tài	too (much)
11.	自己	p, adv	zìjǐ	oneself, by oneself
12.	积极	adj	jījí	positive, enthusiastic
13.	唱歌(儿)	v-o	chànggē(r)	to sing
14.	跳舞	v-o	tiàowǔ	to dance
15.	一定	adv	yīdìng	definitely, certainly
16.	国歌(儿)	n	guógē(r)	national anthem
17.	教书	v-o	jiāoshū	to teach

Text (simplified characters)

I

高文　你在这儿念书念得怎么样？

小张　念得很高兴。我特别喜欢学汉语。

　高　你喜欢看书还是写字？

　张　我喜欢写字。

　高　你现在写得快不快？

　张　不快，我写得很慢。我说话也说得很慢。老师常说我们说话说
　　　得太慢。

　高　我的日语老师也说我们（说话）说得太慢。是不是他们自己说
　　　得太快？

　张　你说得很对。他们有时候儿也太积极，是不是？

II

毛美文　你是不是喜欢唱歌，跳舞？

谢新民　我喜欢唱歌，不喜欢跳舞。

　毛　他们都跟我说你唱歌唱得很好。

　谢　哪里！我唱得不好，但是喜欢唱。你们美国人一定都喜欢跳舞，
　　　是不是？

　毛　不一定，不都喜欢，但是我很喜欢。我常常跟朋友一起跳舞。我
　　　也喜欢唱歌儿。你教我一两个中国歌儿，好不好？

　谢　好，你要学什么歌儿呢？

　毛　你教我你们的国歌儿吧！

New Words (simplified characters)

1.	了	par	le	completion particle
2.	这么	adv	zènme	so, this way
3.	晚	adj	wǎn	late
4.	昨天	n	zuótiān	yesterday
5.	已经	adv	yǐjīng	already
6.	早	adj	zǎo	early
7.	那么	adv	nènme	that way
8.	才	adv	cái	not...until, belatedly
9.	年级	n	niánjí	year (class in school)
10.	下	pref	xià	next
11.	学期	n	xuéqī	school term
12.	开始	v	kāishǐ	to begin
13.	参加	v	cānjiā	to participate
14.	晚会	n	wǎnhuì	evening party
15.	吃	v	chī	to eat
16.	东西	n	dōngxi	thing
17.	玩儿	v	wár	to play, to have fun
18.	还	adv	hái	yet, in addition to
*19.	哈佛	n	Hǎfó	Harvard

---

*An asterisk before a word in the table of new words indicates that the item appears in the pattern sentences of the <u>Companion Book</u>.

I

小谢　今天的报来了没有？

小张　还没〔有〕来呢！

　谢　今天为什么来得这么晚？昨天这〔个〕时候儿已经来了，是不是？

　张　今天是星期二。星期一，三，五来得早，二，四，六来得晚。

　谢　那么星期日呢？

　张　星期日也来得很晚。有时候十点半才来。

II

　谢　你们学了写字没有？

　张　还没学呢！

　谢　小高他们已经学了，你们为什么还没学呢？

　张　他们是二年级的，我们是一年级的。

　谢　你们什么时候儿才学呢？

　张　我们下〔个〕学期开始。

III

高文　你参加了前天的晚会没有？

小张　〔我〕没有〔参加〕。你们呢？

　高　我们去了。很有意思。

　张　你们跳了舞没有？

　高　我跳了，我跳了两个舞。她没跳，她跟朋友们说了很多话。
　　　我们还吃了不少东西，玩儿得很高兴。

LESSON XII

New Words (simplified characters)

1.	遇见	v	yùjian		to meet someone (by chance)
2.	大家	p	dàjiā		all, everybody
3.	哦	int	ò		oh
4.	认识	v	rènshi		to recognize, to be acquainted with
5.	听	v	tīng		to listen
6.	不错	adj	bùcuò		pretty good
7.	句	m	jù		M for sentences
8.	就	adv	jiù		then
9.	走	v	zǒu		to go away, to walk
10.	明天	n	míngtiān		tomorrow
11.	晚上	n	wǎnshang		evening
12.	晚饭	n	wǎnfàn		evening meal
13.	句子	n	jùzi		sentence
14.	讲	v	jiǎng		to explain
15.	清楚	adj	qīngchu		clear
16.	复习	v	fùxí		to review
17.	语法	n	yǔfǎ		grammar
18.	课文	n	kèwén	(课)	text
19.	生词	n	shēngcí		vocabulary (new word)
*20.	念	v	niàn		to read out loud

Text (simplified characters)

I

常学思　毛美文来了没有？

小张　还没〔来〕呢！她两点半来。现在才两点过五分，是不是？

常　对。我昨天在她那儿遇见了一个中国人。

张　那个人叫什么名字？

常　我没有问他。大家都叫他小谢。

张　哦，你遇见了谢新民。我认识他。他唱歌儿唱得很好。你们听了
他唱歌儿没有？

常　听了。昨天他唱了三个歌儿，都唱得很不错。

张　你跟他说了话没有？

常　只说了两句话。他很忙，唱了歌儿就走了。

张　我很喜欢跟他说话。明天晚上吃了晚饭我就到他那儿去，跟他说
说话。你去不去？

常　去。我也去看看他。

II

常学思　今天的练习有八个句子，你作了几个了？

小张　〔我〕作了四个了。

常　你会作后边儿的那四个吗？

张　老师讲得很清楚，我会作。我现在复习复习生词。复习了生词就
作那些句子。

常　你今天也复习语法和课文吗？

张　也复习。作了那些句子就复习语法和课文。

LESSON XIII

New Words (simplified characters)

1.	会	op	huì	can, likely to (could)
2.	汉字	n	Hànzì	Chinese characters
3.	没关系		méiguānxi	(it) does not matter
4.	以后	adv	yǐhòu	in the future
5.	得	op	děi	to have to
6.	字典	n	zìdiǎn	dictionary
7.	能	op	néng	can
8.	想	op	xiǎng	to wish to, to think
9.	打	v	dǎ	to play, to hit
10.	球	n	qiú	ball
11.	后天	n	hòutian	day after tomorrow
12.	考试	n, v	kǎoshì	examination, test
13.	准备	v	zhǔnbèi	to prepare
14.	应该	op	yīnggāi	should
15.	努力	adj	nǔlì	diligent
16.	办法	n	bànfa	way (to deal with difficulty)
17.	非常	adv	fēicháng	extremely, very (much)
18.	可以	op	kěyǐ	may
19.	找	v	zhǎo	to look for, to seek...out
20.	地	par	de	structural particle
21.	不用	op	bùyòng	don't have to

Text (simplified characters)

I

小谢　你现在会不会写汉字？

小张　会，但是写得很慢，也写得不好看。

谢　没关系，以后会写得很好看。

张　老师也这么说。我要好好儿地练习练习。

谢　你听得快不快？

张　还听得很慢。老师还得说得很慢。

谢　你们会用字典不会？

张　不会，现在还不会，以后要慢慢儿地学。现在只要能听，能说，能看，能写。

II

高文　你想不想去打球？

小张　我很想打球，但是今天不能打。

高　为什么呢？

张　下午得好好儿地念书。后天有个日语考试，我得准备准备。

高　我们不应该太努力，有时候儿也该玩儿玩儿。

张　你说得很对，但是有什么办法呢？

高　我有个好办法：我有个日本朋友非常喜欢打球。我们可以找他跟我们一起打球，我们也可以跟他练习练习日语。

张　这个办法不错。他会不会太忙，不能来？

高　我们去找找他。

LESSON XIV

New Words (simplified characters)

1.	同学	n	tóngxué	schoolmate
2.	演	v	yǎn	to act, to present (a play)
3.	话剧	n	huàjù	play
4.	注意	v	zhùyì	to pay attention to
5.	上	pref	shàng	previous, last
6.	通知	n	tōngzhī	notice
7.	因为...所以	conj	yīnwèi...suǒyǐ	because...therefore
8.	交	v	jiāo	to hand in
9.	报告	n	bàogào	report
10.	别的	p	biéde	others
11.	事情	n	shìqing (件)	matter, affair
12.	家	n	jiā	family, home
13.	有名	adj	yǒumíng	famous
14.	不停地	adv	bùtíngde	unceasingly
15.	鼓掌	v	gǔzhǎng	to clap hands
16.	休息	v	xiūxi	to rest
17.	重要	adj	zhòngyào	important
18.	掌握	v	zhǎngwò	to master, to understand thoroughly
19.	意思	n	yìsi	meaning
20.	讨论	v	tǎolùn	to discuss

高文　你看了同学们前天演的那个话剧没有？

张力　什么话剧？

高　　你没有注意他们上星期给我们的那个通知吧？

张　　我这两天因为要交一个报告，所以很忙，没有注意别的事情。他们演的话剧叫什么名字？

高　　叫"家"。

张　　这个话剧很有名。他们演得怎么样？

高　　非常好。大家看了以后都不停地鼓掌。你的报告交了没有？

张　　还没呢！明天可以交。没写以前不知道要用这么多时候儿。

高　　明天你交了报告以后，应该休息休息。

张　　我也想休息休息，但是我还得作那个日语练习呢！很多重要的地方我还没有掌握，可以问你吗？

高　　可以。有一两个句子的意思我也不清楚，我们一起讨论讨论吧！

LESSON XV

New Words (simplified characters)

1.	买	v	mǎi	to buy
2.	汉英	n	Hàn-Yīng	Chinese-English
3.	当然	adv	dāngrán	of course
4.	拿	v	ná	to take, to pick up
5.	种	m	zhǒng	kind
6.	有用	adj	yǒuyòng	useful
7.	合作社	n	hézuòshè	co-op
8.	卖	v	mài	sell
9.	每	sp	měi	each, every
10.	上课	v-o	shàngkè	to attend/to hold a class
11.	从...到	mk	cóng...dào	from...to
12.	就	adv	jiù	(already)
13.	问题	n	wèntí	question
14.	回答	v	huídá	to answer
15.	有的	p	yǒude	some
16.	怎么办		zěnmebàn	What is there to do?
17.	告诉	v	gàosu	to tell (a person)
18.	必须	op	bìxū	should, must
19.	互相	adv	hùxiāng	mutually
20.	要是...就	conj	yàoshi...jiù...	if...then...
21.	方法	n	fāngfa	method, way (of doing things)

Text (simplified characters)

I

毛美文　你昨天买的那本汉英字典，我可以看看吗？

张力　当然可以。在桌子上。你自己拿吧！

毛　　〔看字典〕这种字典很有用。我也应该有一本。

张　　你要是想买，就得快快儿地去买。合作社里的人说，现在买这种字典的人很多。

毛　　我不想买新的。这儿有没有卖旧字典的地方？

张　　我不知道。你可以问问小谢，他知道很多卖旧书的地方。

II

小谢　他们每天什么时候儿上中文课？

张力　他们从一点过五分到两点上中文课。

谢　　他们什么时候儿才开始说话？

张　　他们已经开始了，他们九月就开始了。

谢　　上课的时候儿，他们能说中国话吗？

张　　能说。老师问问题，他们回答。

谢　　老师问的问题，他们都能回答吗？

张　　有的他们能回答，有的他们不能回答。

谢　　要是不能回答，怎么办呢？

张　　要是他们不能回答，他们的老师就告诉他们。

谢　　每个学生老师都问吗？

张　　都问。每个人都必须回答。

谢　　学生们自己也互相问问题吗？

张　　有时候儿互相问问题，有时候儿一起讨论课文里的意思，这是学习的好方法。

LESSON XVI

New Words (simplified characters)

1.	课本	n	kèběn			textbook
2.	着	v	zháo			to reach (as RC)
3.	刚	adv	gāng			just
4.	完	v	wán			to finish
5.	东方	n	dōngfāng			east, eastern
6.	书店	n	shūdiàn	（家，个）		bookstore
7.	也许	adv	yěxǔ			maybe
8.	看见	v	kànjian			to see
9.	开会	v-o	kāihuì			to hold a meeting
10.	请	v	qǐng			to ask, to invite
11.	当	v	dāng			to be, to act as
12.	主席	n	zhǔxí			chairperson
13.	件	m	jiàn			measure word
14.	听见	v	tīngjian			to hear
15.	别人	p	biéren			others (other people)
16.	水平	n	shuǐpíng			level of proficiency
17.	低	adj	dī			low
18.	行	v	xíng			to be good enough, will do
*19.	高	adj	gāo			high

Text (simplified characters)

I

张力1 字典和汉语课本都买着了吗?

毛美文1 课本买着了,字典没买着。我去得太完了,他们刚卖完。

张力2 你可以到东方书店去看看,那儿也许有。

毛美文2 好,我作完练习就去。

II

高文1 你今天看见了毛美文沒有?

张力1 沒有。你要找她吗?

高2 对了。我要问她一件事,下(个)星期开讨论会,我想问她能不能当主席。

张2 上星期我听见她跟别人说她每天三点钟以后,都在合作社工作。你要是去那儿,一定可以找着她。

高3 我昨天去了,但是沒找着她。合作社的人说她昨天沒去。

张3 毛美文也许太忙。你为什么一定要找她当主席呢?你自己当吧!

高4 我的日文水平太低。你来,怎么样?

张4 我也不行。还是请毛美文好。

LESSON XVII

New Words (simplified characters)

1.	站	v	zhàn	to stand
2.	门口(儿)	n	ménkǒu(r)	entrance, doorway
3.	坐	v	zuò	to sit
4.	热	adj	rè	hot
5.	觉得	v	juéde	to feel
6.	有(一)点儿	adv	yǒu(yī)diǎr	somewhat
7.	头	n	tóu	head
8.	疼	v	téng	to ache
9.	脸	n	liǎn	face
10.	红	adj	hóng	red
11.	开	v	kāi	open
12.	窗户	n	chuānghu	window
13.	试	v	shì	to try
14.	坏	adj	huài	bad, broken, out of order
15.	差不多	adv	chàbuduō	almost
16.	完全	adv	wánquán	completely
17.	看	v	kàn	(It) depends (on)
18.	几	nu	jǐ	a few, some
19.	借	v	jiè	to borrow, to lend
20.	成	v	chéng	to succeed (in) to become
21.	极了	inten	jíle	extremely

I

张力　你为什么要站在门口儿？

小谢　我坐的地方太热了。我觉得有（一）点儿不舒服，有（一）点
　　　儿头疼。

张　你的脸很红。你为什么不开开窗户呢？

谢　我试了，但是开不开，也许坏了。

张　我这儿不热，你要不要坐到这儿来？

谢　可以吗？我可以坐在你旁边儿的那把椅子上吗？

张　当然可以，我拿开我的东西。

II

高文　你那个报告今天写得完写不完？

张力　差不多写好了，现在完全要看今天上午看得见看不见毛美文了。

高　为什么呢？

张　我要在报告里写几个汉字，想借毛美文的那枝好毛笔。要是看不
　　见毛美文，当然就借不到毛笔。要是借不到毛笔，那几个汉字就
　　写不成，这个报告也就写不完了。

高　你看，毛美文来了。

张　好极了。我这个报告今天写得完了。

LESSON XVIII

New Words (simplified characters)

1.	回	v	huí		to return
2.	收音机	n	shōuyīnjī	（架，个）	radio
3.	带	v	dài		to bring along
4.	进	v	jìn		to enter
5.	搬	v	bān		to move (one's residence)
6.	间	m	jiān		M for rooms
7.	屋子	n	wūzi	（间）	room
8.	欢迎	v	huānyíng		to welcome
9.	山	n	shān	（座）	hill, mountain
10.	便宜	adj	piányi		inexpensive
11.	城(里)	n	chéng(lǐ)		(in the) city
12.	公共汽车	n	gōnggòngqìchē	（辆）	bus (public car)
13.	费	v	fèi		to take a lot (money, time)
14.	时间	n	shíjiān		time
15.	出	v	chū		to go out
16.	倒是	adv	dàoshi		admittedly so
17.	方便	adj	fāngbiàn		convenient
18.	骑	v	qí		to sit astride
19.	自行车	n	zìxíngchē	（辆）	bicycle
*20.	辆	m	liàng		M for vehicles

张力　毛美文，你回来了。收音机买来了没有？

毛美文　买来了。还带来了一个人。你看，谁进来了？

张力　小谢！你怎么来了？

谢新民　我在店里遇见了毛美文。她告诉我你们这儿有一个人搬走了。我想搬来，所以来看看那间屋子。

张　好。我带你去看看。

（张和谢看了屋子以后回来了。）

毛　怎么样？你喜欢吗？

谢　那间屋子小是小，但是很干净。我非常喜欢。我想下月一号就搬来，行不行？

张　当然行。欢迎你搬来。但是你山上的那个地方很大很便宜，你为什么要搬到城里来呢？

谢　那个地方好是好，但是我每天得坐公共汽车来上课，很费时间，所以想搬到这儿来。

张　这儿出来进去倒是方便。

谢　你们每天怎么去学校？是骑自行车去还是走去？

毛　我走去，小张骑自行车去。

LESSON XIX

New Words (simplified characters)

1.	啊	int	à	ah!
2.	就是	v	jiùshi	to be exactly
3.	谈话	v	tánhuà	to talk, to converse
4.	住	v	zhù	to live, to stay
5.	台北	n	Táiběi	Taipei
6.	忘	v	wàng	to forget
7.	到	v	dào	to reach, to arrive
8.	习惯	v, n	xíguàn	to be used to, habit, custom
9.	父亲	n	fùqin	father
10.	母亲	n	mǔqin	mother
11.	哥哥	n	gēge	elder brother
12.	弟弟	n	dìdi	younger brother
13.	姐姐	n	jiějie	elder sister
14.	妹妹	n	mèimei	younger sister
15.	父母	n	fùmǔ	parents
16.	大夫	n	dàifu	doctor
17.	教师	n	jiàoshī	teacher (as a profession)
18.	刚才	adv	gāngcái	a moment ago
19.	客气	adj	kèqi	polite, modest
20.	楼	m	lóu	(nth) floor (in a building)

高文遇见了谢新民

高　你是从中国来的吗？

谢　是。我是两个月以前才从北京来的。

高　我叫高文。高兴的高，中文的文。你叫什么名字？

谢　我姓谢，我叫谢新民。

高　啊！你就是小谢！毛美文谈话的时候儿常常谈到你。你也住在这儿吗？

谢　对了，我是昨天晚上才搬来的。你的中国话说得很好，是在这个大
　　学学的吗？

高　不是，是三年前在台北学的，已经忘了不少了。你喜欢美国吗？

谢　刚到的时候儿很不习惯，现在好了。

高　你家里有几个人？

谢　我家（里）有父亲，母亲，一个哥哥，一个弟弟。

高　没有姐姐，妹妹吗？

谢　没有。

高　你父母工作不工作？

谢　都工作。我父亲是大夫，我母亲是英文教师。

高　刚才我听见你英文说得很好，现在我知道为什么了。你是跟你母亲学
　　的英文吧？

谢　不是。我是在北〔京〕大〔学〕学的。我说得不好，还得跟你们学习。

高　你太客气。我们以后可以常常谈话了。你住在几楼？

谢　我住在四楼，你呢？

高　我住在二楼。

LESSON XX

New Words (simplified characters)

1.	打	v	dǎ	to hit, to strike
2.	电话	n	diànhuà	telephone
3.	喂	int	wèi	hello!
4.	奇怪	adv	qíguài	strange, feel strange
5.	叫	v	jiào	to order someone to, to ask
6.	对不起	v	duìbuqǐ	I am sorry
7.	发烧	v-o	fāshāo	to run a temperature
8.	一点儿	m	yìdiǎr	a little
9.	感冒	v	gǎnmào	to have a cold
10.	药	n	yào	medicine
11.	片(儿)	m	piàn(r)	a piece
12.	止痛片	n	zhǐtòngpiàn	analgesic tablet (aspirin)
13.	病	v, n	bìng	to be sick; illness
14.	发展	v	fāzhǎn	to develop
15.	医院	n	yīyuàn	hospital
16.	走路	v-o	zǒulù	to walk
17.	了	v	liǎo	to be able to
18.	开车	v-o	kāichē	to drive (a car)
19.	再见	v	zàijiàn	(to see you again) goodbye
20.	一会儿	n	yìhuǐr	in a moment

Text (simplified characters)

打电话

张力　喂，小谢在吗？我要找小谢说话。

谢新民　我就是。你是小张吧！有什么事情？

张　今天上午你没有来唱歌，大家都很奇怪，叫我打电话来问问你。

谢　我今天头疼，所以没去。对不起！

张　你发烧不发烧？

谢　我有一点儿烧。我想我感冒了。

张　你吃了药没有？

谢　我吃了两片止痛片，但是没有用。

张　你应该看看大夫。

谢　感冒是小病，在家里休息休息就可以了。

张　不，感冒有时候儿会发展成大病，特别是有烧的时候儿。

谢　我不认识大夫，怎么办呢？

张　学校的医院大夫很多很好。你可以到那儿去看看。

谢　我现在头疼，走不了路，还是在家休息休息吧！

张　我开车带你去。我五分钟以后就来，好吗？

谢　好吧！谢谢你了。

张　没关系，不谢。再见，一会儿见。

LESSON XXI

New Words (simplified characters)

1.	给	fv	gěi		for, to
2.	信	n	xìn	(封)	letter
3.	病人	n	bìngrén		patient
4.	或者	conj	huòzhě		(either)...or
5.	多	nu	duō		an indefinite number
6.	热情	adj	rèqíng		warm, compassionate
7.	对	prep	duì		to, towards
8.	还	v	huán		to return (things borrowed)
9.	并且	conj	bìngqiě		also, as well
10.	替	fv	tì		for
11.	送	v	sòng		to take...to a place
12.	决定	v	juédìng		to decide
13.	搞	v	gǎo		to engage in, to do
14.	小说(儿)	n	xiǎoshuō(r)		novel
15.	—史	suf	–shǐ		history of...
16.	翻译	v	fānyì		to translate
17.	冷	adj	lěng		cold
18.	希望	v	xīwàng		to hope
19.	身体	n	shēntǐ		health, body
20.	祝	v	zhù		to wish (you...)

Text (simplified characters)

大哥：
三弟：

很长时间没有给你们写信了。你们都好吧？

上星期我病了，住了四天的医院。回来以后休息了两天。今天觉得差不多好了。明天或者后天可以上课了。

这两个多月里，我认识了十多个美国朋友。他们都很热情，都对我很好。我在医院里的时候儿，他们每天都去看我，并且给我作很多事情，替我买东西，替我还书。进医院的时候儿，也是他们送我去的。

我已经决定搞美国小说史了。这儿的图书馆新书很多，杂志也多，非常方便。

父亲母亲都好吗？父亲的病人多不多？母亲的英文小说翻译好了没有？

现在冷了，希望大家注意身体，并且常常写信！

祝

好！

新民
一月十号

LESSON XXII

New Words (simplified characters)

1.	过	v	guò		to pass by (a suffix)
2.	就要...了		jiùyào...le		about to...
3.	春节	n	chūnjié		spring festival
4.	它	p	tā		it
5.	一样	v	yīyàng		to be the same
6.	象	adj	xiàng		to resemble
7.	圣诞节	n	Shèngdànjié		Christmas
8.	放假	v	fàngjià		to have vacation
9.	儿女	n	érnǚ		children (of parents)
10.	别	op	bié		don't...
11.	错	v	cuò		to be wrong
12.	请	v	qǐng		to ask
13.	次	m	cì		time (M for episodes)
14.	筷子	n	kuàizi		chopsticks
15.	难	adj	nán		difficult
16.	饿	adj	è		hungry
17.	家	m	jiā		M for business operations
18.	饭馆儿	n	fànguǎn(r)	(家)	restaurant
19.	菜	n	cài		dish (cooked)
20.	南方	n	nánfāng		southern

Text (simplified characters)

I

小张　时间过得很快。二月就要来了。今年的第一个月已经要过完了。

小谢　对了，春节也快要到了。

张　什么是春节？

谢　春节就是中国的旧新年。我们也叫它春节。

张　春节是几月几号？

谢　每年都不一样。今年是二月四号。

张　中国人怎么过春节？

谢　象你们过圣诞节一样。那天每个地方都放假，儿女们都到父母家去，大家都高高兴兴地玩儿一天，吃一天。

张　春节那天我看见中国人的时候儿应该说什么？

谢　你可以说，"春节好！"也可以说，"祝你春节好。"

张　"春节好…祝你春节好。"我得好好儿地练习练习，四号那天别说错了。

II

谢新民　下星期六是春节，我准备请你在中国城吃饭。你在中国城吃过饭吗？

高文　吃过一次，并且是用筷子吃的。

谢　用筷子吃中国饭难不难？

高　不难，我用过很多次，但是太饿的时候儿我不用。

谢　你去的那家饭馆叫什么名字？菜好不好？

高　是一个南方饭馆，菜很不错。名字我忘了。

LESSON XXIII

New Words (simplified characters)

1.	正	adv	zhèng		progressive expression: happen to be
2.	天气	n	tiānqi		weather
3.	暖和	adj	nuǎnhe		warm
4.	穿	v	chuān		to wear, to put on
5.	着	par	zhe		--ing
6.	大衣	n	dàyī	（件）	overcoat
7.	冬天	n	dōngtian		winter
8.	真	adv, adj	zhēn		really, real
9.	比	fv	bǐ		than, compare
10.	让	fv	ràng		let, make
11.	下雪	v-o	xiàxuě		to snow
12.	刮风	v-o	guāfēng		to blow (wind)
13.	春天	n	chūntian		spring
14.	好象	adv	hǎoxiàng		(it) seems to be
15.	过去	v	guòqu		to go over, to pass by
16.	夏天	n	xiàtian		summer
17.	去年	n	qùnián		last year
18.	秋天	n	qiūtian		autumn
19.	下雨	v-o	xiàyǔ		to rain
20.	漂亮	adj	piàoliang		pretty
21.	男	adj	nán		male
22.	女	adj	nǚ		female

I

谢新民　请进!

高文　你正在忙吗?

谢　没有,我正在看这本翻译小说儿呢!

高　今天天气很暖和。要不要出去走走?

谢　好啊!我也正想出去看看呢!不是很暖和吗?你为什么还穿着大衣呢?

高　暖和是暖和,还没有那么暖和呢!

II

谢　这儿的冬天真不短啊!

高　北京的冬天没有这儿这么长吧?

谢　不,有时候儿也长极了。

高　下雪下得很多吗?

谢　下雪下得不比这儿多,但是常刮大风。刮风的时候儿很不舒服。

高　春天怎么样?

谢　春天很短,有时候儿好象冬天才过去,夏天就来了。这儿夏天热不热?

高　不一定,有时候儿很热。

谢　去年我来的时候儿,正是秋天,天气真好。让我觉得跟在北京一样。

高　秋天要是不下雨,倒是很漂亮。你喜欢春天还是喜欢秋天?

谢　我喜欢秋天。

高　我跟你不一样。我觉得春天比秋天好。èi，那边儿站着的两个人
　　是谁？
谢　你说的是那两个男的吗？
高　不，我说的是那边儿（的）那两个女的。一个好象是毛美文。我
　　们过去看看，好不好？
谢　好。

LESSON XXIV

New Words (simplified characters)

1.	同时	adv	tóngshí		simultaneously
2.	散步	v-o	sànbù		to take a walk
3.	介绍	v	jièshao		to introduce
4.	小姐	n	xiǎojiě		Miss
5.	生活	n	shēnghuó		(daily) life, living
6.	比方说	conj	bǐfāngshuō		for instance
7.	认为	v	rènwéi		to consider, to have a strong opinion of (think)
8.	感觉	v, n	gǎnjué		to feel, feeling
9.	立刻	adv	lìkè		right away
10.	街	n	jiē	(条)	street
11.	人口	n	rénkǒu		population
12.	...分之...	m	...fēnzhī...		...parts of...
13.	就是	conj	jiùshi		it's just that, only
14.	体重	n	tǐzhòng		body weight
15.	增加	v	zēngjiā		to increase
16.	从前	adv	cóngqián		formerly, before
17.	从...起	adv	cóng (TW) qǐ		since or beginning (time)
18.	发现	v	fāxiàn		to discover
19.	发生	v	fāshēng		to occur, to come up

高文，谢新民（同时）　　毛美文！

毛美文　你们也在散步吗？来，我给你们介绍介绍。这是高文，这是谢
　　　　新民。
　　　　我们都叫他小谢。这位是史家明小姐，两个星期以前才从台北来
　　　　的，也是我刚认识的朋友。

高
谢　　（同时）　　　你好！
史

谢　你习惯不习惯这儿的生活？

史　已经很习惯了。台北很多地方象美国一样。

高　我认为台北有很多地方跟美国不一样。

史　当然不完全一样。比方说，这儿走路的人比台北少。

谢　我刚来的时候儿，感（觉）到的第一件事情也是这个。觉得街上
　　的人比中国少得多。

史　美国的人口只有中国的四分之一。街上走路的人当然也比中国少
　　了。

毛　并且，美国人开车的时候儿比走路多。我们走路走得太少了。高
　　文，你这几天怎么样？

高　别的都好，就是体重增加了不少，所以现在每天散步。

毛　你从前没有体重的问题，现在怎么有这个问题了？

高　现在吃得比以前多一点儿了。

毛　为什么呢？

高　从上月发现了一家中国饭馆儿起，我就常常吃中国饭，问题立刻
　　就发生了。

谢　你为什么不少吃一点儿呢？

高　那就是我的问题啊！

LESSON XXV

New Words (simplified characters)

1.	最	adv	zuì		the most
2.	困难	n, adj	kùnnan		difficulty, difficult
3.	容易	adj	róngyi		easy
4.	记	v	jì		to remember, to record
5.	更	adv	gèng		even more
6.	有人	p	yǒurén		some people
7.	简单	adj	jiǎndān		simple
8.	复杂	adj	fǔzá		complicated
9.	简化	v	jiǎnhuà		simplified, to simplify
10.	简体	n	jiǎntǐ		simplified style
11.	笔画	n	bǐhuà	(笔)	strokes
12.	比较	adj	bǐjiǎo		comparatively
13.	繁体	n	fántǐ		complicated style
14.	所有的	p	suǒyǒude		all
15.	钟头	n	zhōngtóu		hour
16.	虽然	conj	suīrán		although
17.	前头	n	qiántou		front
18.	画儿	n	huàr		picture
19.	认	v	rèn		to try to recognize
20.	可不是吗？		ké bushì ma?		exactly!

高文和毛美文讨论写汉字。下边儿是他们的谈话：

高　你觉得学中文最大的困难是什么？

毛　是汉字。

高　你喜欢写字吗？

毛　喜欢。我最喜欢写字了。但是汉字不容易记，也不容易写。

高　有人告诉过我，现在汉字有两种了：一种是简单的，一种是复杂的，对不对？

毛　对。一种是简化的汉字，叫简化字，笔画比较少，也比较容易写。一种是旧汉字，叫繁体字，笔画多，比较难写。

高　是不是所有的汉字都简化了呢？

毛　不，简体字比繁体字少得多。

高　要是两种都得会写，写字就更难了，是不是？

毛　可不是吗？但是汉字很好看，所以我还是喜欢写。

高　你喜欢写简体字还是繁体字呢？

毛　很难说。简体字虽然容易写，但是没有繁体字那么好看。繁体字笔画虽然复杂，但是比简体字好看得多。

高　你们写字，所有的字都得写得一样大吗？

毛　对了。老师开始的时候就告诉我们了：所有的字都应该写得一样大。

高　你写几个字给我看看，好不好？

毛　好...你看，我写了四个字，写得不好，写得不一样大。第四个写得太大了，比前头的三个大得多。

高　你写得真好看，每个字都象一个画儿。我以前只学过说话，没有学过认字写字。以后我也要学学写字了。

LESSON XXVI

New Words (simplified characters)

1.	日记	n	rìjì	diary
2.	毛衣	n	máoyī	sweater
3.	衣服	n	yīfu	garment
4.	浅	adv	qiǎn	light (in color, shade)
5.	绿	adj	lǜ	green
6.	黄	adj	huáng	yellow
7.	白	adj	bái	white
8.	深	adv	shēn	deep (in color, shade)
9.	蓝	adj	lán	blue
10.	样子	n	yàngzi	style, shape
11.	颜色	n	yánse	color
12.	块	m	kuài	piece
13.	点心	n	diǎnxin	refreshment, pastry
14.	爱	v	ài	to like, to love
15.	厕所	n	cèsuǒ	toilet
16.	脚步	n	jiǎobù	footstep
17.	声音	n	shēngyīn	noise, sound
18.	安静	v-o	ānjìng	quiet
19.	搬家	v-o	bānjiā	to move one's residence
20.	同志	n	tóngzhì	comrade (a general title for men and women)
21.	表	n	biǎo	watch
22.	也...也	conj	yě...yě	both...and

Text (simplified characters)

小谢的日记

一月十一号

到美国来了快五个月了。今天第一次一个人进城去买东西。街上的人很不少，但是没有北京那么多。

毛衣穿坏了，想去买一件新的，但是没买成。虽然现在才一月，但是所有的地方都已经开始卖夏天的衣服了。毛衣很少，并且不是浅红的，浅绿的，就是浅黄的，或者白的。我想买一件黑的，或者深蓝的，但是他们说没有。他们说圣诞节以前，样子也多，颜色也多。

高文刚才来了，给我带了来一块点心。这个人别的都好，就是不喜欢学习，自己不爱看书，也不让别人看书。

这间屋子在厕所旁边，脚步的声音真多。我想我还得搬一次家。下星期到老黄那儿去看看，他那儿好象很安静。

友和*让应**同志给我带来了一个表。表很好。但是也让我更想她们了。

*Yǒuhé: a given name

**Yīng: a surname

-143-

LESSON XXVII

New Words (simplified characters)

1.	把	fv	bǎ	to take hold of
2.	糟糕	int	zāogāo	oh dear (what a mess)
3.	送	v	sòng	to give as a present
4.	圆珠笔	n	yuánzhūbǐ	ball-point pen
5.	丢	v	diū	to lose
6.	再	adv	zài	again, once more
7.	不好意思	adj	bùhǎoyìsi	embarrassing, embarrassed
8.	生产	v	shēngchǎn	to produce
9.	工厂	n	gōngchǎng	factory
10.	咳	int	hài	sound of regret or mild disgust
11.	停	v	tíng	to park (a car)
12.	自来水	n	zìláishuǐ	running water
13.	洗	v	xǐ	to wash
14.	百	nu	bǎi	hundred
15.	块	m	kuài	dollar
16.	钱	n	qián	money
17.	讲话	n	jiǎnghuà	lecture
18.	大意	n	dàyì	general idea
19.	怕	v	pà	to be afraid (of)
20.	哎呀	int	āiyā	oh dear
21.	教室	n	jiàoshǐ	classroom

I

谢新民　糟糕！我把小张送给我的圆珠笔丢了。
毛美文　你可以请他再给你一枝。
　谢　不好意思吧？
　毛　没关系。他家有个生产圆珠笔的工厂。每年都生产得太多，所以他和他哥哥都把太多的送给朋友。
　谢　咳！我不知道，不好意思了半天！

II

　谢　谁把车停在这儿了？
　高　我。这是我的车。
　谢　你为什么把车开到这儿来？
　高　因为这儿有自来水。我想把车洗一洗。
　谢　为什么要洗车？
　高　我要用钱，想把车卖了。没卖以前，把它洗干净了，也许可以多卖一百块钱。

III

　毛　今天上午我没能去上课。你能不能把老师讲话的大意告诉我？
　高　他的讲话很复杂。我怕记不住，所以把他说的话都记在本子上了。你可以看看。
　毛　好。你的本子呢？
　高　在这儿…哎呀，糟糕，我把本子忘在教室里了！

LESSON XXVIII

New Words (simplified characters)

1.	座	m	zuò	M for buildings or massive objects
2.	房子	n	fángzi	house
3.	大楼	n	dàlóu	tall building
4.	又...又		yòu...yòu	not only...but also
5.	亮	adj	liàng	bright
6.	房钱	n	fángqián	rent
7.	贵	adj	guì	expensive
8.	付	v	fù	to pay
9.	除了...以外		chúle...yǐwài	except, besides
10.	电费	n	diànfèi	electricity charge (fee)
11.	毛	m	máo	dime
12.	分	m	fēn	cent
13.	空气	n	kōngqì	air
14.	缺点	n	quēdiǎn	drawback
15.	睡	v	shuì	to sleep
16.	起	v	qǐ	to get up
17.	关(上)	v	guān (shang)	to turn off
18.	附近	n	fùjìn	vicinity
19.	合适	adj	héshì	suitable, fitting
20.	服务员	n	fúwùyuán	attendant
21.	一共	adv	yīgòng	altogether
22.	找	v	zhǎo	to give change to

Text (simplified characters)

I

谢新民　老黄，我觉得你这座房子比我住的那个大楼好得多。你的屋子
　　　又干净又亮，这两个窗户真大。

黄　但是房钱贵啊!

谢　你每〔个〕月付多少房钱?

黄　一个月二百零五块〔钱〕。

谢　只比我多五块钱，不到百分之三。

黄　但是我除了房钱以外，还得付电费呢!

谢　电费多少钱一个月?

黄　电费两个月付一次。每次二十二块两毛五分钱。

谢　但是你的屋子很安静，空气也好。

黄　除了有点儿贵以外，这个地方还有一个缺点。这儿住的人除了
　　我以外，都不是学生，都喜欢早睡早起。每天十一点以后，一定
　　要把收音机关上。

谢　现在我才知道，你这儿不比我那儿好。在学校附近要找到合适的
　　房子真不容易。

II

服务员1　您要买什么？

学生1　你们有圆珠笔吗？

服务员2　有，都在这儿。我们有一块钱一枝的，有五毛钱一枝的，也有两毛五分钱一枝的。您要哪种？

学生2　我试试。...这种五毛钱一枝的不错。

服务员3　对了。又好看又便宜。

学生3　好，我要一枝。那些英汉字典一本多少钱？

服务员4　九块五一本。

学生4　有没有便宜一点儿的？

服务员5　这本小（一）点儿的比较便宜，六块七毛五一本。

学生5　好。我买一本绿的。一共多少钱？

服务员6　一共七块两毛五。...您给了十块钱，我找您两块七毛五。

学生6　好。再见。

服务员7　再见。

New Words (simplified characters)

1.	表演	v	biǎoyǎn	to give a performance
2.	春假	n	chūnjià	spring vacation
3.	计划	n	jìhuà	plan
4.	查	v	chá	to look up (information)
5.	论文	n	lùnwén	thesis
6.	提前	adv	tíqián	ahead of schedule
7.	完成	v	wánchéng	to complete
8.	可惜	v	kěxī	too bad
9.	不然	conj	bùrán	otherwise
10.	纽约	n	Niǔyuē	New York City
11.	音乐	n	yīnyuè	music
12.	什么的	p	shénmede	and so forth
13.	旅行	v	lǚxíng	to travel
14.	批评	v	pīping	to criticize
15.	一天到晚	adv	yītiān dàowǎn	all day long, all the time
16.	睡觉	v-o	shuìjiào	to sleep
17.	不但...而且	conj	bùdàn...érqiě	not only...but also
18.	老	adv	lǎo	keep on (doing something)
19.	一边(儿)... 一边(儿)	conj	yībiān(r)...yībiān(r)	V1 while V2
20.	大声(儿)	adv	dàshēng(r)	loudly
21.	干	v	gàn	to do (same as 作)

Text (simplified characters)

高文　小谢，去年你表演了一次唱歌儿。今年还表演吗？
谢新民　今年不表演了。
　高　我很喜欢听唱歌儿。我真希望你再表演一次。
　谢　我现在没有时间搞这些了。
　高　下星期放春假，你有什么计划？想出去玩儿玩儿吗？
　谢　我不能出去，我得在图书馆里查查书。我希望能把论文提前完成。
　高　你不应该不休息啊！可惜我已经把车卖了。不然我一定带你到纽约去玩儿玩儿，去听听音乐，吃吃中国饭，看看话剧，什么的。
　谢　老黄买了新车。你可以找他一起去。
　高　我不想再跟老黄一起旅行了。他太爱批评人。去年我跟他一起旅行的时候儿，他一天到晚批评我。不是说我开车开得太快，就是说我睡觉睡得太多。他自己呢？不但吃得很多，而且老一边儿吃一边儿大声儿〔地〕说话。我不喜欢这种批评人的人。
　谢　那么你现在正在干什么呢？
　高　我…我…我…

LESSON XXX

New Words (simplified characters)

1.	早	adj	zǎo	good morning
2.	太太	n	tàitai	Mrs., wife
3.	先生	n	xiānsheng	Mr., husband
4.	流利	adj	liúlì	fluent
5.	最近	adv	zuìjìn	recently, recent
6.	又	adv	yòu	again
7.	下儿	m	xiàr	M for action
8.	关心	v	guānxīn	to be concerned about
9.	听说	v	tīngshuō	to have heard people say
10.	一天比一天		yītiān bǐ yītiān	day by day
11.	提高	v	tígāo	to raise
12.	情况	n	qíngkuàng	condition
13.	算是	adv	suànshi	to be considered as
14.	进步	adj	jìnbù	improved, progressive
15.	许多	adj	xǔduō	many, lots of
16.	需要	v	xūyào	to need
17.	解决	v	jiějué	to solve
18.	国家	n	guójiā	country, nation
19.	恐怕	adv	kǒngpà	I am afraid that
20.	得很	int	--dehěn	extremely

谢新民　您早！白太太。

白太太　您早！谢先生。您是什么时候来美国的？

谢　我是半年前来的。您的中国话说得真流利。

白　哪里哪里！我以前去过中国。

谢　您是什么时候儿去的？

白　三十多年以前。在中国住过两年。

谢　您最近又去过没有？

白　没有。回来（了）以后没有再去过，但是我非常关心中国。听说中国现在发展得很快。每个人都有饭吃，有衣服穿。生活水平也一天比一天提高了。

谢　现在的情况算是比从前进步了，但是生产上还有许多问题需要解决。

白　我希望能跟您多谈谈。下星期四您有没有时间来参加一个晚会？我希望您能把您国家最近的情况给大家介绍一下儿。

谢　对不起。我最近有点儿忙。下星期要到纽约去两天。恐怕没时间参加晚会。对不起得很！

白　没关系。我以后再请您。

LESSON XXXI

New Words (simplified characters)

1.	用不着	v	yòngbuzháo	unneeded, to have no need for
2.	放	v	fàng	to put
3.	安排	v	ānpái	to arrange
4.	够	adj	gòu	enough
5.	最好	adv	zuìhǎo	it would be best
6.	重	adj	zhòng	heavy
7.	推	v	tuī	to push
8.	主意	n	zhúyi (zhǔyi)	idea
9.	墙	n	qiáng	wall
10.	掉	v	diào	to fall off
11.	难看	adj	nánkàn	ugly
12.	相片(儿)	n	xiàngpiān(r)	photograph
13.	挂	v	guà	to hang up
14.	糖	n	táng	sugar, candy
15.	水果	n	shuǐguǒ	fruit
16.	帮助	v	bāngzhù	to help
17.	录音带	n	lùyīndài	audiotape
18.	跑	v	pǎo	to run
19.	发音	n	fāyīn	pronunciation

晚会以前

小张　今天晚上的晚会有多少人参加？

毛美文　有五，六十人吧！我们应该把用不着的东西放回去，把桌子椅子安排一下儿。椅子够不够？

张　不够。最好能把门外边儿的那张大椅子搬进来。

毛　我们可以试试。

张　我想太重了，我们两个人搬不进来。

毛　再找一个人来一起搬。三个人就搬得进来了。

张　再把这两把小椅子搬过去，把门旁边儿的大桌子推过来一点儿。

毛　这个主意不错。把大桌子推过来以后，大家走出去走进来就方便得多了。

张　你看，墙上的那张画儿快掉下来了。那张画儿又旧又难看。

毛　把它拿下来，把你屋子里的那张大相片挂上去，怎么样？

张　好。我们开始吧！

毛　刚才买的糖和水果还在车里呢！我去把那些东西拿进来。你去找一下儿史家明。请她帮助我们。

张　她在哪儿呢？

毛　我走下楼来的时候儿，她正拿着很多录音带跑上楼去。她一定在屋子里练习发音呢！

New Words (simplified characters)

1.	吸烟	v-o	xīyān		to smoke
2.	台	m	tái		measure word
3.	电视(机)	n	diànshì(jī)	（台）	television (set)
4.	修理	v	xiūli		to repair
5.	紧张	adj	jǐnzhāng		tense
6.	对	prep	duì		toward, to
7.	组织	v	zǔzhi		to organize
8.	克服	v	kèfú		to overcome
9.	工夫	n	gōngfu		free time
10.	好处	n	hǎochu		advantage
11.	自在	adj	zìzai		comfortable, at ease
12.	节目	n	jiému		program
13.	简直	adv	jiǎnzhí		simply
14.	包	m, v	bāo		package, to wrap up
15.	茶	n	chá		tea
16.	喝	v	hē		to drink
17.	杯	m	bēi		cupful
18.	法国	n	Fǎguó (Fàguó)		France
19.	酒	n	jiǔ		wine, liquor
20.	又...了	adv	yòu...le		again(!)

谢新民   高文，你不是早就决定不吸烟了吗？怎么今天又吸起来了？

高文   我刚把这台电视机修理好，修理得太紧张了。现在想看看电视，
吸吸烟，休息一下儿。

谢   看起来不吸烟很难，但是我觉得你应该想出一个办法来。这样吸
下去，对身体不好。

高   这件事说起来容易，作起来难。

谢   不少人都有这个问题。也许你应该把这儿所有的吸烟的人都组织
起来，大家互相帮助，克服你们的困难。

高   你想出来的办法好是好，但是谁有工夫呢？并且，吸烟有时候儿
也有好处。像今天吧，又刮风，又下雨。也不能散步，也不能打
球。（要是）不吸烟能干什么呢？

谢   看电视还不够自在吗？

高   这些节目很没有意思。吸着烟看，还看得下去，不吸烟，简直看
不下去。

谢   我想起来了：我上星期买了一包绿茶，我请你喝一杯中国茶。

高   谢谢你。要是你有法国酒就更好了！

LESSON XXXIII

New Words (simplified characters)

1.	早上	n	zǎoshang	morning
2.	雨衣	n	yǔyī	raincoat
3.	小心	adj	xiǎoxīn	careful
4.	早饭	n	zǎofàn	breakfast
5.	百货大楼	n	bǎihuòdàlóu	department store
6.	一块儿	adv	yīkuàr	together
7.	最后	adv	zuìhòu	finally
8.	午饭	n	wǔfàn	lunch
9.	各	sp	gè	each, various
10.	躺	v	tǎng	to lie down
11.	床	n	chuáng	bed
12.	预告	n	yùgào	forecast
13.	笑	v	xiào	to laugh, to smile
14.	记得	v	jìde	to remember
15.	提	v	tí	to mention
16.	机会	n	jīhui	chance, opportunity
17.	小时	n	xiǎoshí	hour

高文进城

春天到了，差不多天天下雨，街上人人都穿着雨衣。高文去年不小心，把雨衣丢了。今天早上，他决定再买一件。吃完了早饭就进城去了。

快到百货大楼的时候儿，高文遇见了一个从前的同屋。他也是去买雨衣的。他们就说着话一块儿走进了百货大楼，找到卖雨衣的地方。雨衣的样子真不少，件件都很漂亮。他们看了半天，试了好几件，最后每人买了一件，在一起吃了午饭，就各人回到各人的学校去了。

高文走进（他）屋子的时候儿，他同屋正躺在床上听天气预告呢！一看见高文，他就说："明天又要下雨了。"高文说："没关系，我雨衣已经买来了。"说完，就把雨衣拿出来给他同屋看。他同屋一看就笑起来了。他说："我也买了一件完完全全一样的。"高文问他："你用了多少钱？"他同屋说："我用了五十九块九毛五。你呢？"高文说："我不告诉你。"他同屋说："我看出来了：我买得比你便宜，是不是？"

高文说："对了。我知道我不应该在城里买东西。我记得你以前提过，合作社里的东西比较便宜。但是今天早上我不想念书，想找个机会到城里去看看，看看城里有没有新东西卖，所以很早就进城去了。"

"那么城里有没有新东西卖呢？"他的同屋问。

"我没注意。我遇见了一个朋友，跟他说了一个多小时的话，忘了注意这件事了。"

LESSON XXXIV

New Words (simplified characters)

1.	...室	suf	...shǐ	(a) room for...
2.	近代	n	jìndài	modern period
3.	思想	n	sīxiǎng	thoughts
4.	玛立	n	Mǎlì	woman's name -- Mary
5.	研究	v	yánjiu	to do research in
6.	五四	n	wǔsì	May Fourth
7.	运动	n	yùndòng	movement
8.	题目	n	tímu	topic
9.	越...越	conj	yuè...yuè	the more...the more
10.	生日	n	shēngrì	birthday
11.	礼物	n	lǐwu	gift
12.	唱片(儿)	n	chàngpiān(r)	record
13.	文化	n	wénhuà	culture
14.	民间	n	mínjiān	folk, popular (among people)
15.	故事	n	gùshi	story
16.	语言	n	yǔyán	language
17.	学院	n	xuéyuàn	institute
18.	为	fv	wèi	for the sake of, in order to
19.	年轻	adj	niánqīng	young
20.	岁	n	suì	years of age
21.	头发	n	tóufa	hair

在学生休息室里

I

谢新民　《中国近代思想史》。这本书是谁的？

高文　是玛立的。她最近研究起五四运动来了。她说这个题目越研究越有意思。今年夏天还要研究下去呢！

谢　玛立这会儿是不是不在这儿？

高　她去打电话〔去〕了。你要找她吗？她一会儿就回来。

谢　不。我找你。送给她的生日礼物，你想出来了没有？

高　我已经买了。我买了一张唱片儿——一张新出来的唱片儿。我希望她喜欢。你买了什么？

谢　我还没想出来呢！我越想越拿不定主意。你替我想想。

高　她喜欢中国文化。你可以给她买一本中国民间故事书。

谢　你想得真好。这个主意不错。我一会儿就去买。

II

谢　毛美文，听说你要到北京语言学院去工作了。我真为你高兴。

毛　我非常高兴。可惜北京我没有朋友。

谢　我大哥家在语言学院附近。到了北京，你可以去找找他。

毛　那好极了。你大哥象你一样吗？

谢　他很喜欢朋友，特别是年轻的朋友。

毛　你大哥今年多大？

谢　他比我大五岁，快四十岁了。

毛　你已经三十多了吗？我没有看出来。你看上去和我们一样大。

谢　不，我比你们大得多。你看，我已经有白头发了。

LESSON XXXV

New Words (simplified characters)

1.	夜里	n	yèli	in the night
2.	连...也/都		lián...yě/dou	even...
3.	对不住	v	duìbuzhù	to be sorry (to be unable to face someone)
4.	害	v	hài	to cause
5.	一直	adv	yīzhí	continuously, all along
6.	中学	n	zhōngxué	high school
7.	西方	n	xīfāng	western
8.	从来	adv	cónglái	all along
9.	千	nu	qiān	thousand
10.	专业	n	zhuānyè	field of concentration
11.	历史	n	lìshǐ	history
12.	方面	n	fāngmian	respect, aspect
13.	请教	v	qǐngjiào	to ask for instruction or advice
14.	选	v	xuǎn	to elect
15.	门	m	mén	M for academic courses
16.	文学	n	wénxué	literature
17.	如果	conj	rúguǒ	if
18.	解释	v	jiěshi	explain
19.	只要...就	conj	zhǐyào...jiù	so long as, if only

玛立　小谢，你给我的那本书，我越看越放不下。昨天夜里看了半本，连觉都差不多没睡。

谢　太对不住了，害你没睡觉。你真那么喜欢那些故事吗？

玛　非常喜欢。我一直很爱看民间故事。在中学的时候儿，只要有工夫，我就到图书馆去看民间故事的书。连最简单的我也看，所以西方的故事看了不少，但是从来没看过东方的民间故事。中国有四千多年的文化，民间故事一定很多。

谢　这儿的图书馆里这种书多得很。

玛　好极了。我的专业是中国历史，所以应该多看一些这方面的书。中国历史有些地方我不太清楚，以后可以请教你吗？

谢　别说请教。只要我知道，我一定告诉你。我这学期选了一门美国文学史，以后在英文方面如果有问题，也要请你解释解释呢！

玛　好，我们互相帮助，互相学习吧！

LESSON XXXVI

New Words (simplified characters)

1.	问路	v	wènlù	to ask for directions
2.	请问	v	qǐngwèn	Please, may I ask...
3.	火车	n	huǒchē	train
4.	站	suf	zhàn	station
5.	离	pre	lí	from
6.	远	adj	yuǎn	far
7.	路	n	lù	road, route (no.__)
8.	多	adv	duō (duó)	how
9.	近	adj	jìn	near
10.	往	fv	wàng	toward
11.	街口儿	n	jiēkǒur	intersection (of streets)
12.	转	v	zhuǎn	turn
13.	条	m	tiáo	M for streets
14.	邮局	n	yóujú	post office
15.	公园(儿)	n	gōngyuán(r)	park
16.	花儿	n	huār	flowers
17.	校园(儿)	n	xiàoyuán(r)	schoolyard
18.	经过	v	jīngguò	to pass by
19.	迎春	n	yíngchūn	forsythia
20.	大概	adv	dàgài	probably
21.	感到	v	gǎndao	to feel
22.	永远	adv	yǒngyuǎn	forever
23.	有诗意	adj	yǒushīyì	poetic

I

问路

A 1　请问，去火车站怎么走？

B 1　火车站离这儿很远，最好坐二十二路公共汽车去。

A 2　公共汽车站离这儿有多远？

B 2　公共汽车站离这儿比较近。从这儿往前走，走到前头的街口儿，
往左转，再往前走，过了两条街，你就会看见个邮局。过了邮局，
你就可以看见个公园儿。公共汽车站就在公园儿的前边儿。

A 3　谢谢！谢谢！

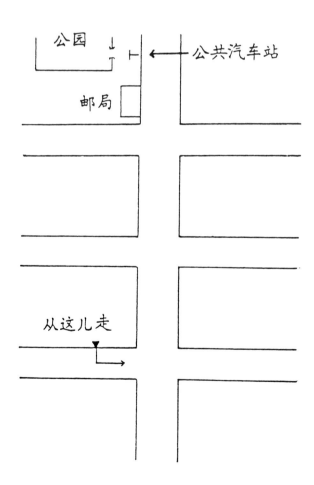

II

看花儿

高文　今天天气多么暖和啊！我们到校园儿里去散散步吧！

史家明　好吧！昨天经过大图书馆的时候儿，看见很多迎春花儿已经黄了，今天这么暖和，大概已经开开了吧！

高　　我们去看看吧！你喜欢迎春吗？

史　　喜欢，你呢？

高　　我也很喜欢。很多人都喜欢这种花儿。我想这是因为迎春开得最早。大家经过了一个很长的冬天以后，看见了一些黄黄的花儿，都感到特别高兴。

史　　我想迎春这个名字很好。"迎"是欢迎的意思，"春"当然是春天。"欢迎春天"，多（么）有意思啊！别的花儿的名字，我常常记不住，但是迎春这个名字我永远忘不了。这个名字多么有诗意啊！

LESSON XXXVII

New Words (simplified characters)

1.	周末	n	zhōumò	weekend
2.	华盛顿	n	Huáshèngdùn	Washington
3.	参观	v	cānguān	to visit (a place)
4.	各处	n	gèchù	various places
5.	戏	n	xì	play
6.	满意	v	mǎnyì	to be satisfied
7.	本来	adv	běnlái	originally
8.	音乐会	n	yīnyuèhuì	concert
9.	座位	n	zuòwei	seat
10.	让	fv	ràng	by
11.	只好	adv	zhǐhǎo	have no choice but to
12.	演员	n	yǎnyuán	actor, actress
13.	第一流	adj	dìyīliú	first-rate
14.	被	fv	bèi	by
15.	海	n	hǎi	sea
16.	英里	m	yīnglǐ	mile
17.	游泳	v	yóuyǒng	to swim
18.	样儿	n	yàngr	style
19.	杯子	n	bēizi	cup, glass
20.	衬衫	n	chènshān	shirt, blouse
21.	累	adj	lèi	tired
22.	以为	v	yǐwéi	to think wrongly (thought)
23.	可是	conj	kěshi	but

玛立　小谢，你周末玩儿了还是念书了？

谢新民　玩儿了。前天从华盛顿来了一个老同学。他要参观我们的大学。我带他到各处去走了走。昨天下午看了一个戏。

玛　〔戏〕看得怎么样？

谢　看得一点儿也不满意。我本来是想带他去听音乐会的，但是决定得太晚，好的座位都让人买去了，所以只好去看戏。他们说那些演员都是第一流的，但是我觉得他们演得一点儿也不好。你干了什么了？

玛　我被一个朋友请去，在海边儿上玩儿了一天。

谢　这时候儿去海边儿，不冷吗？

玛　我也以为会冷。没想到一点儿也不冷。我们是骑车去的，骑了二十多英里，骑得有一点儿热。

谢　你们游泳了没有？

玛　没有。我们只散散步，在各处看看。我朋友的哥哥在离海边儿不远的地方开了一个店。我们到那个店里去买了一些东西。他们的东西卖得真便宜。你看，这样儿的杯子才两块五毛钱一个。

谢　你穿着的衬衫很漂亮，也是在那儿买的吗？

玛　对了。才九块钱一件。多便宜！

谢　听上去你周末过得很好。

玛　可是我昨天骑车骑得太多了。今天觉得很累。一点儿也不想工作，老想睡觉。

LESSON XXXVIII

New Words (simplified characters)

1.	毕业	v, n	bìyè	to graduate, graduation
2.	典礼	n	diǎnlǐ	ceremony
3.	举行	v	jǔxíng	to hold a ceremony
4.	万	nu, n	wàn	ten thousand, a surname
5.	祖父	n	zǔfù	grandfather
6.	旅馆	n	lǚguǎn	hotel
7.	满	adj	mǎn	full
8.	爱人	n	àiren	husband, wife
9.	定	v	dìng	to reserve
10.	房间	n	fángjiān	room
11.	校友	n	xiàoyǒu	alumnus/a
12.	造船	v-o	zàochuán	to make ships, ship building
13.	公司	n	gōngsī	company
14.	等…再	adv	děng…zài	wait until
15.	结果	adv	jiéguǒ	as a result
16.	照相	v-o	zhàoxiàng	to take pictures
17.	票(子)	n	piào(zi)	ticket
18.	上海	n	Shànghǎi	Shanghai
19.	代表	v	dàibiǎo	to represent
20.	饱	adj	bǎo	full (from eating)

高文　这两天校园里人真多。大概校友们都回来参加毕业典礼了。

张力　毕业典礼哪天举行？

高　　星期四，就是后天。我的同屋万大为今年毕业。他家里的人昨天就已经来了。连他（的）八十多岁的祖父也来了。

张　　哦，所以各处的旅馆都住得那么满！上星期我要替我弟弟和他的爱人定一个房间，打了很多电话，怎么定也定不着。所有的旅馆都说，"一个房间也沒有了，连最贵的房间也被人定去了。"

高　　你弟弟他们也要来参加毕业典礼吗？

张　　不，他们要来参观一家造船公司的，现在他们决定等下个月再来了。

高　　你去不去看毕业典礼呢？

张　　我不去。你想去吗？

高　　我一定得去。张友文给了我一张票子。他家里的人都在上海，当然不能来看他毕业了。

张　　你应该去，你可以代表他家里的人。但是最好早早儿地去。有一年，老黄的女朋友毕业，老黄去了。典礼九点才开始，虽然他八点半就到了校园，可是已经连一个座位也沒有了。他说人真多，他怎么找也找不着座位。最后是站在大图书馆前边看的。结果，什么也看不清楚，连相都沒照成。所以，你得早早儿地去，别象老黄那年一样。

LESSON XXXIX

New Words (simplified characters)

1.	好久不见		hǎojiǔbujiàn	Haven't seen you for a long time
2.	见面	v-o	jiànmiàn	to see each other
3.	呀	int	yā	interjection particle
4.	生病	v-o	shēngbìng	to be sick
5.	飞机	n	fēijī	airplane
6.	中国民航	n	Zhōngguómínháng	CAAC (Chinese airline)
7.	东京	n	Dōngjīng	Tokyo
8.	先...再	adv	xiān...zài	first...then
9.	飞机场	n	fēijīchǎng	airport
10.	等	v	děng	to wait
11.	糊涂	adj	hútu	muddle-headed
12.	上	v	shàng	to board (a vehicle)
13.	公路	n	gōnglù	highway
14.	定	v	dìng	to set, settled
15.	号	n	hào	number (ordinal)
16.	班机	n	bānjī	flight
17.	通	v	tōng	to communicate by letter, telephone, etc.
18.	啦	par	la	rhetorical particle
19.	见	v	jiàn	to see
20.	帮忙	v-o	bāngmáng	to help

Text (simplified characters)

喂，喂，...我就是。你是老黄吧！...我一听就听出来是你。好久不见！我们有两个月没有见面了吧？...我呀？我这几天哪儿也没去。我的车让弟弟给借去了，今天才还我的。你怎么样？...什么？你要回台北去？...　　哦！你母亲生什么病？...哦。你什么时候走？...坐哪家公司的飞机？...坐中国民航的飞机？中国民航的飞机到得了台北吗？...哦，你先到东京，再坐日航...éi，这个主意不错。...你在东京飞机场要等多少时候呢？...要等四个半钟头？太长了！你在东京有朋友吗？...哦，大为在东京，我忘了。你看我多〔么〕糊涂！...你明天晚上就走？有人送你上飞机场吗？...我送你去飞机场，怎么样？...没关系，你不用去找别人了。...不，不，那是去年的事。我现在已经不怕开公路了，现在哪儿都能去了。...好，说定了。我明天一定送你。...你要我几点去我就几点去，什么时候都行。...可以，可以。...没关系，我明天一定五点钟到你那儿。...好，好。〔你〕有什么别的事我可以帮忙吗？...大为知道你坐几号班机吗？...哦，你们已经通过电话啦？好极了。...好，好。明天见...明天见！

LESSON XL

New Words (simplified characters)

1.	留学	v	liúxué	to study abroad
2.	封	m	fēng	M for letter
3.	亲爱	adj	qīn'ài	dear
4.	时差	n	shíchā	time difference
5.	离开	v	líkāi	to leave
6.	高	adj	gāo	tall
7.	对于	prep	duìyú	to, in
8.	兴趣	n	xìngqu	interest
9.	醒	v	xǐng	to wake up
10.	下	v	xià	to get off, dismount
11.	将来	adv	jiānglái	in the future
12.	印象	n	yìnxiàng	impression
13.	深	adj	shēn	deep
14.	青年	n	qīngnián	youth
15.	自由	adj	zìyóu	freedom
16.	活泼	adj	huópo	lively
17.	友谊	n	yǒuyí	friendship
18.	不断地	adv	bùduànde	unceasingly
19.	增长	v	zēngzhǎng	to grow
20.	交流	n	jiāoliú	exchange
21.	起...作用	v	qǐ...zuòyong	to produce...effect
22.	单元	n	dānyuán	apartment

23.	厨房	n	chúfáng	kitchen
24.	卫生间	n	wèishēngjiān	bathroom (hygiene room)
25.	热烈	adv	rèliè	heartily
26.	快乐	adj	kuàilè	happy
27.	女儿	n	nǚ'er	daughter

谢新民在美国留学了一年，上个月回国去了。下边儿是他回国以后写来的第一封信：

亲爱的同学们，

我到家已经快一个月了，大概因为时差吧：我一直觉得很累，老觉得睡不够，所以今天才给你们写信。对不起得很！

中国和一年前差不多，但是我的女儿比我离开的时候高得多了。她对于你们给她的小火车特别有兴趣，天天一醒就下床去找她的火车。她说她将来要坐火车到美国去呢！

过去一年里，我认为给我印象最深的是美国青年了。你们不但思想自由，活泼，而且对朋友也非常热情。你们给我的帮助是我永远忘不了的。我希望我们的友谊能不断地增长，能在中美两国（的）文化交流上起一些作用。

下月我们要搬家了，要搬进一个大一点儿的单元去。除了厨房，卫生间以外，还有三间大屋子。玛立来了以后，一定要在我们家住几天。我和我爱人都热烈地欢迎你来住。

我爱人要谢谢你们。你们送给她的那本书，对于她的工作非常有用。

今天我就写这些了，别的下次再写。希望我们能常常通信。

祝你们

快乐！

小谢
六月十二号

Glossary Index

Chinese - English

pīnyīn	traditional characters	simplified characters	meaning in English	lessons

A

pīnyīn	traditional characters	simplified characters	meaning in English	lessons
ā	啊		ah!	19
āi-yā	哎呀		oh!	27
ài	愛	爱	like, love	31
àiren	愛人	爱～	husband, wife	38
ānjìng	安静	～静	quiet	26
ānpái	安排		arrange	31

B

pīnyīn	traditional characters	simplified characters	meaning in English	lessons
ba	吧		suggestion particle	6
bā	八		eight	4
bǎ	把		measure word	5
bǎ	把		to take hold of	27
bái	白		white	26
bǎi	百		hundred	27
bǎihuòdàlóu	百货大樓	～货～楼	department store	33
bān	搬		to move	18
bānjiā	搬家		to move residence	26
bānjī	班機	～机	flight	39
bàn	半		half	7
bànfa	辦法	办～	way (to deal with (difficulty)	13
bāngmáng	幫忙	帮～	to help	39

bāngzhù	幫助	帮～	to help	31
bāo	包		package	32
bǎo	飽	饱	full (from eating)	32
bào	報	报	newspaper	1
bàogào	報告	报～	report	14
bēi	杯		cupful	32
bēizi	杯子		cup, glass	37
Běijīng	北京		Beijing (Peking)	2
bèi	被		by	37
běn	本		measure word	2
běnzi	本子		notebook	3
běnlái	本來	～来	originally	37
bǐ	比		than	23
bǐfangshuō	比方説	～～说	for instance	24
bǐhuà	筆畫	笔画	strokes	25
bǐjiǎo	比較	～较	comparatively	25
bìxū	必須	～须	should, must	15
bìyè	畢業	毕业	to graduate, graduation	38
biǎo	錶	表	watch	26
biǎoyǎn	表演		to give a performance	29
bié	別		don't	22
biéde	別的		others	14
biéren	別人		other people	16
bìng	病		sick	20
bìngren	病人		patient	21
bìngqiě	並且	并～	furthermore, also	21
bùcuò	不錯	～错	pretty good	12
bùdàn...érqiě	不但...而且		not only...but also	29
bùduànde	不斷地	～断～	unceasingly	40

bù	不		no, not	1
bùhǎoyìsi	不好意思		embarrassing, embarrassed	27
bùrán	不然		otherwise	29
bùtíngde	不停地		unceasingly	14
bùyòng	不用		don't have to	13

C

cái	才		not until, only	11
cài	菜		(cooked) dish of food	22
cānguān	參觀	参观	to visit (a place)	37
cānjiā	參加	参～	to participate	11
cèsuǒ	廁所	厕～	toilet	26
chá	查		to look things up	29
chá	茶		tea	32
chà	差		be short of	7
chàbuduō	差不多		almost	17
cháng	長	长	long	3
chángcháng	常常		often, most of the time	9
chànggē(r)	唱歌(兒)	～～(儿)	sing	10
chàngpiān(r)	唱片(兒)	～～(儿)	record	34
chènshān	襯衫	衬～	shirt, blouse	37
chéng	成		to become, succeed	17
chénglǐ	城裡	城里	(in the) city	18
chī	吃		to eat	11
chīfàn	吃飯	～饭	to have a meal	11
chū	出		to go out	18
chúfáng	廚房	厨～	kitchen	40

chúle...yǐwài	除了...以外		except, besides	28
chuān	穿		to wear	23
chuānghu	窗戶		window	17
chuáng	牀	床	bed	33
chūnjià	春假		spring vacation	29
chūnjié	春節	～节	spring festival	22
chūntian	春天		spring	23
cì	次		time (M for action)	22
cóng	從	从	from	8
cóng...dào	從...到	从...～	from...to	15
cónglái	從來	从来	all along	35
cóng...qǐ	從...起	从...～	since (time past)	24
cóngqián	從前	从～	formerly, before	24
cuò	錯	错	wrong	22

D

dǎ	打		to play (ball)	13
			to hit, to strike	
dǎ	打		to make (phone calls)	20
dà	大		big	2
dàgài	大概		probably	36
dàjiā	大家		everyone	12
dàlóu	大樓	～楼	tall building	28
dàshēng(r)	大聲(兒)	～声(儿)	loudly	29
dàxué	大學	～学	university, college	6
dàyī	大衣		overcoat	23
dàyì	大意		general idea	27
dài	帶	带	to bring along	18
			(or take with)	

dàibiǎo	代表		to represent	38
dàifu	大夫		doctor	19
dānyuán	單元	单～	apartment	40
dànshi	但是		but	8
dāng	當	当	to be, to act as	16
dāngrán	當然	当～	of course	15
dào...lái/qù	到...來/去	～...来/～	come/go to a place	8
dào	到		reach, arrive	19
dàoshi	倒是		admittedly so	18
de	的		possessive article	3
de	地		structural particle	13
de	得		verb particle	10
dehěn	得很		extremely	30
děi	得		have to, should	13
děng	等		wait	39
děng...zài	等...再		wait until	38
dī	低		low	16
dì	第		ordinal prefix	6
dìdi	弟弟		younger brother	19
dìfang	地方		place	9
dìyīliú	第一流		first-rate	37
diǎnzhōng	點鐘	点钟	o'clock (point on a clock)	7
diǎnlǐ	典禮	～礼	ceremony	38
diǎnxin	點心	点～	refreshment, pastry	26
diàn	店		store	18
diànfèi	電費	电费	electricity charge (fee)	28
diànhuà	電話	电话	telephone	20
diànshì(jī)	電視(機)	电视(机)	television (set)	32
diànyǐng(r)	電影(兒)	电～(儿)	movie	8

diào	掉		to fall	31
dìng	定		to reserve	38
dìng	定		to be settled	39
diūle	丟了		to be lost	27
dōngfāng	東方	东～	east, eastern	26
Dōngjīng	東京	东～	Tokyo	39
dōngtian	冬天		winter	23
dōngxi	東西	东～	thing	11
dǒng	懂		to understand	6
dōu	都		all	5
duǎn	短		short	3
duì	對	对	to, toward	21
duìbuduì	對不對	对～对	(Is it) right?	3
duìbuqǐ	對不起	对～～	I am sorry	20
duìbuzhù	對不住	对～～	I am sorry	35
duìle	對了	对～	(It is) right	3
duìyú	對於	对于	to, in	40
duō	多		many	2
duō	多		indefinite number	21
duō (duó)	多		how	36
duōshǎo	多少		how many, how much	4

E

è	餓	饿	hungry	22
érnǚ	兒女	儿～	children (of parents)	22
èr	二		two	4

F

fāshāo	發燒	发烧	run a temperature	20
fāshēng	發生	发～	occur, come up	24
fāxiàn	發現	发现	discover	24
fāyīn	發音	发～	pronunciation	31
fāzhǎn	發展	发～	develop	20
Fǎguó	法國	～国	France	32
fānyì	翻譯	～译	translate	21
fántǐ	繁體	～体	complicated style	25
fànguǎn	飯館	饭馆	restaurant	22
fāngbiàn	方便		convenient	18
fāngfǎ	方法		method, way (of doing things)	16
fāngmiàn	方面		respect, aspect	35
fángjiān	房間	～间	room	38
fángqián	房錢	～钱	rent	28
fángzi	房子		house	28
fàng	放		put	31
fàngjià	放假		have vacation	22
fēicháng	非常		extremely, very	13
fēijī	飛機	飞机	airplane	39
fēijīchǎng	飛機場	飞机场	airport	39
fèi	費	费	take a lot (time, money)	18
fēn	分		minute	7
fēn	分		cent	28
...fēn zhī...	...分之...		...parts of...	24
fēng	封		M for letters	40
fúwùyuán	服務員	～务员	attendant	28

GC-7

fùzá	複雜	复杂	complicated	25
fù	付		pay	28
fùjìn	附近		vicinity	28
fùmǔ	父母		parents	19
fùqin	父親	～亲	father	19
fùxí	複習	复习	to review	12

G

gānjing	乾淨	干净	clean	3
gǎndào	感到		feel	36
gǎnjué	感覺	～觉	feel	24
gǎnmào	感冒		have a cold	20
gàn	幹	干	do	29
gāng	剛	刚	just	16
gāngbǐ	鋼筆	钢笔	fountain pen	3
gāngcái	剛才	刚～	a moment ago	19
gāo	高		tall, high	40
gāoxìng	高興	～兴	cheerful, glad, happy	10
gǎo	搞		engage in, do	21
gàosu	告訴	～诉	tell (a person)	15
gēge	哥哥		elder brother	19
gè	各		each, various	33
gè	個	个	measure word	2
gèchù	各處	～处	various places	37
gěi	給	给	give	4
gěi	給	给	for, to	21
gēn	跟		and	6
gēn	跟		with	8

gèng	更		even more	25
gōngchǎng	工廠	～厂	factory	27
gōngfu	工夫		free time	32
gōnggòngqìchē	公共汽車	～～～车	bus (public car)	18
gōnglù	公路		highway	39
gōngsī	公司		company	38
gōngyuán(r)	公園(兒)	～园(儿)	park	36
gōngzuò	工作		work, to work	4
gòu	夠		enough	31
gǔzhǎng	鼓掌		clap hands	14
gùshi	故事		story	34
guāfēng	刮風	～风	blow (wind)	23
guà	掛	挂	hang	
guān	關	关	turn off	16/28
guānxīn	關心	关～	be concerned about	30
guì	貴	贵	expensive	28
guìxìng	貴姓	贵～	(What's your) honorable surname?	6
-guó	國	国	suffix (country)	1
guógē(r)	國歌(兒)	国～(儿)	national anthem	10
guójiā	國家	国～	country, nation	30
guò	過	过	past (time)	7
guò	過	过	pass by, a suffix	22
guòqu	過去	过～	go over, pass	23

H

Hǎfó	哈佛		Harvard	11
hái	還	还	yet, in addition to	11
hái	還	还	still	13

háishi	還是	还～	...or...?	5
háishi	還是	还～	after all	16
hǎi	海		sea	37
hài	害		cause	35
hài	咳		sound of mild reproach	27
Hàn-Yīng	漢英	汉～	Chinese-English	15
Hànyǔ	漢語	汉语	Chinese language	5
Hànzì	漢字	汉～	Chinese characters	13
hǎo	好		good	2
hǎochu	好處	～处	advantage	32
hǎohāorde	好好兒地	～～儿～	well	13
hǎojiǔbujiàn	好久不見	～～～見	Haven't seen you for a long time	39
hǎokàn	好看		good-looking	9
hǎoxiàng	好像	～象	it seems that	23
hào	號	号	ordinal day of the month	7
hào	號	号	number (ordinal)	39
hē	喝		drink	32
hé	和		and	5
héshì	合適	～适	suitable, fitting	28
hézuòshè	合作社		cooperative society	15
hēibǎn	黑板		blackboard	3
hěn	很		very	2
hóng	紅	红	red	17
hòubian(r)	後邊(兒)	后边(儿)	back	9
hòutian	後天	后～	day after tomorrow	13
hútu	糊塗	～涂	muddle-headed	39
hùxiāng	互相		mutually	15

Huáshèngdùn	華盛頓	华～顿	Washington	37
huàbào	畫報	画报	pictorial	5
huàjù	話劇	话剧	play	14
huài	壞	坏	bad, broken	17
huānyíng	歡迎	欢～	welcome	18
huán	還	还	return (things borrowed)	21
huáng	黃	黃	huang	26
huār	花兒	～儿	flowers	36
huàr	畫兒	画儿	picture	25
huí	回		return	18
huídá	回答		reply, answer	15
huì	會	会	know, be skillful in	5
huì	會	会	can, likely to	13
huópo	活潑	～泼	lively	40
huǒchē	火車	～车	train	36
huòzhě	或者		(either)...or...	21

J

jīhuì	機會	机会	chance	33
jījí	積極	积极	positive, enthusiastic	10
jíle	極了	极～	extremely	17
jǐ	幾	几	how many	4
jǐ	幾	几	a few, some	17
jì	記	记	remember, record	25
jìde	記得	记～	remember	33
jìhuà	計劃	计划	plan	29
jiā	家		family, home	14
jiā	家		M for business concern	22

jiān	間	间	M for rooms	18
jiǎndān	簡單	简单	simple	25
jiǎnhuà	簡化	简～	simplified	25
jiǎntǐ	簡體	简体	simplified style	25
jiǎnzhí	簡直	简～	simply	32
jiàn	件		measure word	16
jiàn	見	见	see	39
jiànmiàn	見面	见～	see each other	39
jiānglái	將來	将来	in the future	40
jiǎng	講	讲	explain	12
jiǎnghuà	講話	讲话	lecture, speech	27
jiāo	教		teach	4
jiāo	交		hand in	14
jiāoliú	交流		exchange	40
jiāoshū	教書	～书	teach	10
jiǎobù	腳步	脚～	footstep	26
jiào	叫		be called	6
jiào	叫		tell, ask (someone to do something)	20
jiàoshī	教師	～师	teacher	19
jiàoshǐ	教室		classroom	27
jiē	街		street	24
jiēkǒu(r)	街口(兒)	～～(儿)	intersection (of streets)	36
jiéguǒ	結果	结～	as a result	38
jiémù	節目	节～	explain	35
jiějie	姐姐		elder sister	19
jiějué	解決	～决	solve	30
jiěshì	解釋	～释	explain	35
jiè	借		borrow, lend	17

jièshao	介紹	～绍	introduce	24
jīnnián	今年		this year	7
jīntian	今天		today	7
jǐnzhāng	緊張	紧张	tense, nervous	32
jìn	近		near	36
jìn	進	进	enter	18
jìnbù	進步	进～	improved, progressive	30
jìndài	近代		modern period	34
jīngguò	經過	经过	pass by	36
jiǔ	九		nine	4
jiǔ	酒		wine, liquor	32
jiǔ	久		long time	39
jiù	舊	旧	old, used	2
jiù	就		then	12
jiù	就		already	15
jiùshi	就是		be exactly	19
jiùshi	就是		all except	24
jiùyào...le	就要...了		about to	22
jǔxíng	舉行	举～	hold (a ceremony)	38
jù	句		M for sentences	12
jùzi	句子		sentence	12
juéde	覺得	觉～	feel	17
juédìng	決定	决～	decide	21

K

kāi	開	开	open	17
kāichē	開車	开车	drive a car	20
kāihuì	開會	开会	hold a meeting	16
kāishǐ	開始	开～	begin	11

kàn	看		read, look at	4
kàn	看		(it) depends	17
kànjian	看見	～見	see	16
kànshū	看書	～书	read (silently)	10
kǎoshì	考試	～试	examination, test	13
kě bushi ma	可不是嗎	～～～吗	exactly, that's just the way it is	25
kěshi	可是		but	37
kěxí	可惜		too bad	29
kěyǐ	可以		may	13
kè	刻		quarter (of an hour)	7
kè	課	课	lesson	12
kèběn	課本	课～	textbook	16
kèfú	克服		overcome	32
kèqi	客氣	～气	polite	19
kèwén	課文	课～	text	12
kōngqì	空氣	～气	air	28
kǒngpà	恐怕		I am afraid that...	30
kuài	塊	块	M for piece	26
kuài	塊	块	dollar	27
kuài	快		fast	10
kuàilè	快樂	～乐	happy	40
kuàizi	筷子		chopsticks	22
kùnnán	困難	～难	difficulty	25

L

la	啦		rhetorical particle	39
lái	來	来	come	7
lán	藍	蓝	blue	26

lǎo	老		old, of long standing, aged	2
lǎo	老		keep on ...ing	29
lǎoshī	老師	～师	teacher	1
le	了		completion particle	11
lèi	累		tired	37
lěng	冷		cold	21
lí	離	离	from (distance)	36
líkai	離開	离开	leave	40
lǐbian(r)	裡邊(兒)	里边(儿)	inside	9
lǐwù	禮物	礼～	gift	34
lìkè	立刻		right away	24
lìshǐ	歷史	历～	history	35
lián...yě/dōu	連...也/都	连...～/～	even	35
liǎn	臉	脸	face	17
liànxí	練習	练习	exercise, practice	5
liǎng	兩	两	two	2
liàng	亮		bright	28
liàng	輛	辆	M for vehicles	18
liǎo	了		be able to	20
líng	零		zero	7
liúlì	流利		fluent	30
liúxué	留學	～学	study abroad	40
liù	六		six	4
lóu	樓	楼	floor (of a building)	19
lù	路		road, route ____	36
lùyīndài	錄音帶	录～带	audiotape	31
lǚguǎn	旅館	～馆	hotel	38
lǚxíng	旅行		to travel	29
lù	綠	绿	green	26

lùnwén	論文	论～	thesis	29

M

ḿ	呣		what (did you say)?	4
Mǎlì	瑪立	玛～	woman's name - Mary	34
ma	嗎	吗	question particle	1
mǎi	買	买	buy	15
mài	賣	卖	sell	15
mǎn	滿	满	full	38
mǎnyì	滿意	满～	satisfied	37
màn	慢		slow	10
mànmārde	慢慢兒地	～～儿～	slowly	13
máng	忙		busy	7
máo	毛		dime	28
máobǐ	毛筆	～笔	writing brush	3
máoyī	毛衣		sweater	26
méiguānxi	沒關係	～关系	it does not matter	13
méiyou	沒有		have not, be without	2
měi	每		each, every	15
Měiguó	美國	～国	U. S. A.	1
mèimei	妹妹		younger sister	19
mén	門	门	door	17
mén	門	门	M for academic courses	35
ménkǒur	門口兒	门～儿	entrance	17
-men	們	们	suffix (plural pronoun)	3
mínjiān	民間	～间	folk, popular	34
míngtian	明天		tomorrow	12
míngzi	名字		name	6
mǔqin	母親	～亲	mother	19

ná	拿		take, pick up	15
nà	那		that	1
nán	男		male	23
nán	難	难	difficult	22
nánfāng	南方		southern	22
nánkàn	難看	难~	ugly	31
nǎr (nǎli)	哪兒(哪裡)	~儿(~里)	where	8
nàr (nàli)	那兒(那裡)	~儿(~里)	there	8
ne	呢		particle	4
něi	哪		which	6
nèi	那		that	1
nènme	那麼	~么	that much, that way	11
néng	能		can	13
nǐ	你		you	1
nián	年		year	7
niánjí	年級	~级	year (class in school)	11
niánqīng	年輕	~轻	young	34
niàn	念		read aloud	12
niànshū	念書	~书	study, read	10
nín	您		you (polite form)	1
Niǔyuē	紐約	纽约	New York City	29
nǚ	女		female	23
nǚ'ér	女兒	~儿	daughter	40
nǔlì	努力		diligent	13
nuǎnhe(nuǎnhuo)	暖和		warm	23

O

ò	哦		oh (now I know)	12

P

pà	怕		be afraid (of)	27
pángbiān(r)	旁邊(兒)	～边(儿)	side of	9
pǎo	跑		run	31
péngyou	朋友		friend	3
pīpíng	批評	～评	criticize	29
piǎnyi	便宜		inexpensive	18
piàn(r)	片(兒)	～(儿)	measure word	20
piào(zi)	票(子)		ticket	38
piàoliang	漂亮		pretty	23

Q

qī	七		seven	4
qí	騎	骑	sit astride, ride	18
qíguài	奇怪		strange	20
qǐ	起		rise	28
qǐ...zuòyòng	起...作用		produce...effect	40
qiān	千		thousand	35
qiānbǐ	鉛筆	铅笔	pencil	3
qián	錢	钱	money	27
qiánbian(r)	前邊(兒)	～边(儿)	front	9
qiántian	前天		day before yesterday	8
qiántou	前頭	～头	front	25
qiǎn	淺	浅	light	26
qiáng	牆	墙	wall	31

qīn'ài	親愛	亲爱	dear	40
qīngchu	清楚		clear	12
qīngnián	青年		youth	40
qíngkuàng	情況		condition (situation)	30
qǐng	請	请	ask (someone to do something)	16
qǐng	請	请	invite	22
qǐngjiào	請教	请～	ask for advice or instruction	35
qǐngwèn	請問	请问	Please, may I ask	36
qiūtian	秋天		autumn	23
qiú	球		ball	13
qù	去		go	7
qùnian	去年		last year	23
quēdiǎn	缺點	～点	drawback	28

R

ràng	讓	让	let, make	23
ràng	讓	让	by	37
rè	熱	热	hot	17
rèliè	熱烈	热～	heartily	40
rèqíng	熱情	热～	warm, compassionate	21
rén	人		person	1
rénkǒu	人口		population	24
rénmín	人民		people (of a country)	5
rèn	認	认	try to recognize	25
rènshi	認識	认识	recognize	12
rènwéi	認爲	认为	consider, have a strong opinion	24

rì	日		day	7
rìbào	日報	～报	daily (newspaper)	5
Rìběn	日本		Japan	6
rìjì	日記	～记	diary	26
Rìyǔ	日語	～语	Japanese language	5
róngyi	容易		easy	25
rúguǒ	如果		if	35

S

sān	三		three	2
sànbù	散步		to take a walk	24
shān	山		mountain, hill	18
Shānběn	山本		Yamamoto (Japanese surname)	6
shàng	上		previous, last	14
shàng	上		board (a vehicle, plane)	39
shàngbian(r)	上邊(兒)	～边(儿)	top, above	9
Shànghǎi	上海		Shanghai	38
shàngkè	上課	～课	hold class, attend class	15
shàngwǔ	上午		forenoon	8
shǎo	少		few	2
shéi	誰	谁	who	6
shēn	深		dark (color)	26
shēn	深		deep	40
shēntǐ	身體	～体	health, body	21
shénme	甚麼	什么	what	6
shénmede	甚麼的	什么～	and so forth	29
shēngbìng	生病		be sick	39
shēngchǎn	生產	～产	produce	27

shēngcí	生詞	～词	vocabulary (new word)	12
shēnghuó	生活		life	24
shēngrì	生日		birthday	34
shēngyin	聲音	声～	noise, sound	26
Shèngdànjié	聖誕節	圣诞节	Christmas	22
shí	十		ten	4
shíchā	時差	时～	time difference	40
shíhou(r)	時候(兒)	时～(儿)	time	7
shíjiān	時間	时间	time	18
-shǐ	一史		history of	21
-shǐ	一室		room for...	34
shì	是		be	1
shì	試	试	try	17
shìqing	事情		matter, affair	14
shōuyīnjī	收音機	～～机	radio	18
shū	書	书	book	1
shūdiàn	書店	书～	bookstore	16
shūfu	舒服		comfortable	9
shuǐguǒ	水果		fruit	31
shuǐpíng	水平		level of proficiency	16
shuì	睡		sleep	28
shuìjiào	睡覺	～觉	sleep	29
shuōhuà	說話	说话	speak	10
sīxiǎng	思想		thoughts	34
sì	四		four	4
sòng	送		take...to a place	21
sòng	送		give as a present	27
sùshè	宿舍		dormitory	8
suànshi	算是		be considered as	30
suīrán	雖然	虽～	although	25

suì	歲	岁	years of age	34
suǒyǐ	所以		therefore	14
suǒyǒude	所有的		all	25

T

tā	他		he	1
tā	她		she	9
tā	它		it	22
tái	台		measure word	32
Táiběi	台北		Taipei	19
tài	太		too (much)	10
tàitai	太太		Mrs., wife	30
tánhuà	談話	谈话	talk, converse	19
táng	糖		sugar, candy	31
tǎng	躺		lie down	33
tǎolùn	討論	讨论	discuss	14
tèbié	特別		special, unusual	10
téng	疼		ache	17
tí	提		mention	33
tígāo	提高		raise, improve	30
tímù	題目	题~	topic	34
tíqián	提前		ahead of schedule	29
tǐzhòng	體重	体~	(body) weight	24
tì	替		for	21
tiān	天		day	7
tiānqi	天氣	~气	weather	23
tiáo	條	条	M (for streets)	36
tiàowǔ	跳舞		dance	10
tīng	聽	听	listen	12

tīngjian	聽見	听见	to hear	16
tīngshuō	聽説	听说	heard people say	30
tíng	停		park (a car)	27
tōng	通		communicate (by letter, telephone)	39
tōngzhī	通知		notice	14
tóngshí	同時	同时	simultaneously	24
tóngzhì	同志		general title for men and women (comrade)	26
tóngwū	同屋		roommate	6
tóngxué	同學	～学	schoolmate	14
tóu	頭	头	head	17
tóufa	頭髮	头发	hair	34
túshūguǎn	圖書館	图书馆	library	9
tuī	推		push	31

W

wàibian(r)	外邊(兒)	～边(儿)	outside	9
wán	完		finish	16
wánchéng	完成		complete	29
wánquán	完全		completely	17
wǎn	晚		late	11
wǎnfàn	晚飯	～饭	evening meal, supper	12
wǎnhuì	晚會	～会	evening party	11
wǎnshang	晚上		evening	12
wàn	萬	万	ten thousand, surname	38
wàng	往		toward	36
wàng	忘		forget	19
wár	玩兒	～儿	play, have fun	11

wèi	位		M for people	6
wèi	爲	为	for	34
wèi	喂		hello	20
wèishénme	爲甚麼	为什么	why	8
wèishēngjiān	衛生間	卫～间	bathroom (hygiene room)	40
wénhuà	文化		culture	34
wénxué	文學	～学	literature	35
wèn	問	问	ask (a question)	8
wènlù	問路	问～	ask for directions	36
wèntí	問題	问题	question, problem	15
wǒ	我		I, me	1
wūzi	屋子		room	18
wǔ	五		five	4
wǔfàn	午飯	～饭	lunch	33
wǔsì	五四		May Fourth	34

X

xīfang	西方		west, western	35
xīwàng	希望		hope	21
xīyān	吸煙	～烟	smoke	32
xíguàn	習慣	习惯	be used to, habit	19
xǐ	洗		wash	27
xǐhuan	喜歡	～欢	to like	8
xì	戲	戏	play, drama	37
xià	下		next	11
xià	下		get off	40
xiàbian(r)	下邊(兒)	～边(儿)	bottom, below, under	9
xiàtian	夏天		summer	23

xiàwǔ	下午		afternoon	8
xiàxuě	下雪		snow	23
xiàyǔ	下雨		rain	23
xiānsheng	先生		Mr., husband	30
xiān...zài	先...再		first...then	39
xiànzài	現在	现~	now	7
xiǎng	想		wish to, think	13
xiàng	像	象	resemble	22
xiàngpiān(r)	相片(兒)	~~(儿)	photograph	31
xiǎo	小		small	2
xiǎojiě	小姐		Miss	24
xiǎoshí	小時	~时	hour	33
xiǎoshuō(r)	小説(兒)	~说(儿)	novel	21
xiǎoxīn	小心		careful	33
xiào	笑		laugh, smile	33
xiàoyǒu	校友		alumnus/a	38
xiàoyuán	校園	~园	schoolyard	36
xiē	些		a few, some	5
xiězì	寫字	写~	write	10
xièxie	謝謝	谢谢	thank you	4
xīn	新		new	2
xìn	信		letter	21
xīngqī	星期		week	7
xíng	行		to be good enough, will do	16
xǐng	醒		wake up	40
xìng	姓		have the surname of...	6
xìngqu	興趣	兴~	interest	40
xiūli	修理		repair	32
xiūxi	休息		rest	14

xūyào	需要		need	30
xǔduō	許多	许～	many, lots of	30
xuǎn	選	选	elect	35
xué	學	学	to learn (a skill), to study	5
xuéqī	學期	学～	school term	11
xuésheng	學生	学～	student	1
xuéxí	學習	学习	to study	4
xuéxiào	學校	学～	school	5
xuéyuàn	學院	学～	institute	34

Y

yā	呀		interjection particle	39
yánjiu	研究	研究	do research in	34
yánsè	顏色	颜～	color	26
yǎn	演		act in a play	14
yǎnyuán	演員	～员	actor, actress	37
yàngr	樣兒	样儿	kind, style	37
yàngzi	樣子	样～	style, shape	26
yào	要		want to	8
yào	藥	药	medecine	20
yàoshi...(jiù)	要是...(就)		if...(then)	15
yě	也		too, also	4
yě...yě	也...也		both...and	26
yīgòng	一共		altogether	28
yěxǔ	也許	～许	maybe	16
yèli	夜裡	～里	in the night	35
yī	一		one	2
yīfu	衣服		garment	26

yīyuàn	醫院	医院	hospital	20
yīdìng	一定		definitely, certainly	10
yīkuàr	一塊兒	～块儿	together	33
yīxiàr	一下兒	～～儿	a little (action)	31
yīyàng	一樣	～样	be the same	22
yǐhòu	以後	～后	afterwards, in the future	13
yǐjīng	已經	～经	already	11
yǐqián	以前		before, formerly	6
yǐwéi	以爲	～为	think wrongly	37
yǐzi	椅子		chair	5
yībiān(r)...	一邊(兒)...	～边(儿)...	V1 while V2	29
yībiān(r)	一邊(兒)	～边(儿)		
yīdiǎr	一點(兒)	～点(儿)	a little	20
yīhuǐr	一會兒	～会儿	a moment	20
yīqǐ	一起		together	8
yìsi	意思		meaning	14
yītiān bǐ yītiān	一天比一天		day by day	30
yītiān dào wǎn	一天到晚		all day long, all the time	29
yīzhí	一直		continuously, all along	35
yīnwèi...(suóyǐ)	因爲...(所以)	～为...(～～)	because...(therefore)	14
yīnyuè	音樂	～乐	music	29
yīnyuèhuì	音樂會	～乐会	concert	37
yìnxiàng	印象		impression	40
yīnggāi	應該	应该	should	13
Yīngguó	英國	～国	England	3
yīnglǐ	英里		mile	37
Yīngwén	英文		English language	3
yíngchūn	迎春		forsythia	36

yǒngyuǎn	永遠	～远	forever	36
yòng	用		use	5
yòngbuzháo	用不着		unneeded	31
yóujú	郵局	邮～	post office	36
yóuyǒng	游泳		swim	37
yǒu	有		have	2
yǒude	有的		some	15
yǒu(yi)diǎr	有(一)點兒	～(～)点儿	somewhat	17
yǒumíng	有名		famous	14
yǒurén	有人		some (people)	25
yǒushīyì	有詩意	～诗～	poetic	36
yǒushíhou(r)	有時候(兒)	～时～(儿)	sometimes	9
yǒushèr	有事兒	～～儿	not free, busy	8
yǒuyí	友誼	～谊	friendship	40
yǒuyìsi	有意思		interesting	5
yǒuyòng	有用		useful	15
yòubian(r)	右邊(兒)	～边(儿)	right side	9
yòu	又		again	30
yòu...le	又...了		again!	32
yòu...yòu	又...又		not only...but also	28
yǔfǎ	語法	语～	grammar	12
yǔyī	雨衣		raincoat	33
yǔyán	語言	语～	language	34
yùgào	預告	预～	forecast	33
yùjian	遇見	～见	to meet (by chance), to encounter	12
yuánzhūbǐ	圓珠筆	圆～笔	ball-point pen	27
yuǎn	遠	远	far	36
yuè	月		month	7
yuè...yuè	越...越		the more...the more	34

yùndòng	運動	运动	movement	34

Z

zázhì	雜誌	杂志	magazine	9
zài	在		be at (a place)	8
zài	再		again, further	27
zàijiàn	再見	～见	good-bye (see you again)	20
zāogāo	糟糕		oh dear, how terrible	27
zǎo	早		early	11
zǎo	早		good morning	30
zǎofàn	早飯	～饭	breakfast	33
zǎoshang	早上		morning	33
zàochuán	造船		ship building	38
zěnme	怎麼	～么	how	6
zěnmebàn	怎麼辦	～么办	What is there to do?	15
zěnmeyàng	怎麼樣	～么样	how about...	6
zènme	這麼	这么	this much, this way	11
zēngjiā	增加		increase	24
zēngzhǎng	增長	～长	grow, increase	40
zhàn	站		stand	17
-zhàn	站		suffix for station (transportation)	36
zhāng	張	张	measure word, surname	2/3
zhǎngwò	掌握		master, understand thoroughly	14
zháo	着		reach	16
zhǎo	找		look for, seek...out	13
zhàoxiàng	照相		take pictures	38

zhe	着		...ing (particle)	23
zhè	這	这	this	1
zhèi	這	这	this	1
zhēn	真		really, real	23
zhèng	正		(just)...ing	23
zhèr (zhèli)	這兒 (這裡)	这儿(这里)	here	8
zhī	枝		measure word	3
zhīdao	知道		to know	6
zhǐ	只		only	4
zhǐ	紙	纸	paper	2
zhǐhǎo	只好		have no choice but to	37
zhǐtòngpiàn	止痛片		analgesic tablet (aspirin)	20
zhǐyào...jiù	只要...就		so long as	35
Zhōngguó	中國	～国	China	1
Zhōngguómínháng	中國民航	～国～～	Chinese airline (CAAC)	39
zhōngjiàn(r)	中間(兒)	～间(儿)	middle, between, among	9
zhōngtóu	鐘頭	钟头	hour	25
Zhōngwén	中文		Chinese language	3
zhōngxué	中學	～学	high school	35
zhǒng	種	种	kind	15
zhòng	重		heavy	31
zhòngyào	重要		important	14
zhōumò	週末	周～	weekend	37
zhúyi	主意		idea	31
zhǔxí	主席		chairperson	16
zhù	住		live, stay	19
zhù	祝		wish (good wishes)	21

zhùyì	注意		pay attention to	14
zhuānyè	專業	专业	field of concentration	35
zhuǎn	轉	转	turn	36
zhǔnbèi	準備	准备	prepare	13
zhuōzi	桌子		table, desk	5
zìdiǎn	字典		dictionary	13
zìjǐ	自己		oneself	10
zìláishuǐ	自來水	～来～	running water	27
zìxíngchē	自行車	～～车	bicycle	18
zìxué	自學	～学	self-study, to do homework	9
zìyóu	自由		free, freedom	40
zìzài	自在		comfortable, at ease	32
zǒu	走		go away, walk, leave	12
zǒulù	走路		walk	20
zǔfù	祖父		grandfather	38
zǔzhī	組織	组织	organize	32
zuì	最		the most	25
zuìhǎo	最好		it would be best	31
zuìhòu	最後	～后	finally	33
zuìjìn	最近		recent, recently	30
zuótian	昨天		yesterday	11
zuǒbian(r)	左邊(兒)	～边(儿)	left side	9
zuò	作		do, make	5
zuò	坐		sit	17
zuò	座		measure word (for buildings, mountains)	28
zuòwei	座位		seat	37

English to Chinese (Pinyin romanization)

A

English	Pinyin	Lesson No.
a few	jǐ	17
a few (suffix)	xiē	5
a little	yīdiǎr	20
a little	yīxiàr	31
a moment ago	gāngcái	19
able	huì	5
able	néng	13
able (potential complement)	liǎo	20
about to...	jiùyào...le, kuàiyào...le	22
above	shàngbian(r)	9
ache	téng	17
act (in a play)	yǎn	14
act as	dāng	16
active	jījí	10
actor	yǎnyuán	37
actress	yǎnyuán	37
admittedly so	dàoshi	18
advantage	hǎochù	32
affair	shìqing	14
afraid (be afraid of)	pà	7
afraid (I am afraid that)	kǒngpà	30
afternoon	xiàwu	8
afterwards	yǐhòu	13
again	yòu	30
again	zài	27
again!	yòu...le	32
age (years of)	suì	34
aged (old)	lǎo	2
ahead of schedule	tíqián	29
air	kōngqì	28
airplane	feiji	39
airport	fēijīchǎng	39
all	dōu	5
all	suǒyǒude	25
all along (never)	cónglái (bù/méi...)	35
all day long	yītiān dào wǎn	29
all except	jiùshi	24
almost	chàbuduō	17
already	yǐjīng	11
also	bìngqiě	21
also	yě	4
although	suīrán	25
altogether	yīgòng	28
alumnus/a	xiàoyǒu	38
always (all along)	yīzhí	35
America	Měiguó	1

B

blow (wind)	guāfēng	23
blue	lán	26
board, get on	shàng	39
body	shēntǐ	21
body weight	tǐzhòng	24
book	shū	1
bookstore	shūdiàn	16
borrow	jiè	17
both...and	yě...yě	26
bottom	xiàbian(r)	9
breakfast	zǎofàn	33
bright	liàng	28
bring along	dài	18
broken	huài	17
bus	gōnggòngqìchē	18
busy	máng	7
busy	yǒushèr	8
but	dànshi	8
but	kěshì	37
buy	mǎi	15
by	bèi	37
by	jiào	37
by	ràng	37

C

call (be called)	jiào	6
call (on phone)	dǎ (diànhuà)	20
can	huì	13
can	néng	13
candy	táng	31
careful	xiǎoxīn	33
cause (do harm to)	hài	35
cent	fēn	28
ceremony	diǎnlǐ	38
certainly	yídìng	10
chair	yǐzi	5
chairman	zhǔxí	16
chance	jīhuì	33
change (give change to)	zhǎo	28
cheerful	gāoxìng	10
children (of parents)	érnǚ	33
China	Zhōngguó	1
Chinese airline (CAAC)	Zhōngguómínháng	39
Chinese characters	Hànzì	13
Chinese language	Hànyǔ	5
Chinese language	Zhōngwén	3
Chinese-English	Hàn-Yīng	15
chopsticks	kuàizi	22
Christmas	Shèngdànjié	22

D

dear	qīn'ài	40
decide	juédìng	21
deep (color)	shēn	26
deep	shēn	40
definitely	yídìng	10
department store	bǎihuòdàlóu	33
depends (it depends)	kàn	17
deplete	wán	16
desk	zhuōzi	5
develop	fāzhǎn	25
diary	rìjì	26
dictionary	zìdiǎn	13
difficult	kùnnan	25
difficult	nán	22
difficulty	kùnnan	25
diligent	nǔlì	13
diligently	hǎohāorde	13
dime	máo, jiǎo	28
discover	fāxiàn	24
discuss	tǎolùn	14
disposal structure	bǎ	27
do	gàn	29
do (engage in)	gǎo	21
do	zuò	5
do homework	zìxué	9
do research in	yánjiū	34
doctor	dàifu	19
dollar	kuài, yuán	27
don't	bié	22
don't have to	bùyòng	13
door	mén	17
doorway	ménkǒu(r)	17
dormitory	sùshè	8
drawback	quēdiǎn	28
drink	hē	32
drive (a car)	kāichē	20

E

each	gè	33
each	měi	15
early	zǎo	11
east	dōngfāng	16
eastern	dōngfāng	16
easy	róngyi	25
eat	chī	11
eight	bā	4
elder brother	gēge	19
elder sister	jiějie	19
elect	xuǎn	35

electricity charge	diànfèi	28
embarrassed, embarrassing	bùhǎoyìsi	27
engage in	gǎo	21
English language	Yīngwén	3
enough	gòu	31
enter	jìn	18
enthusiastic	jījí	10
even	lián...yě/dōu	35
even more	gèng	25
evening	wǎnshang	12
evening meal	wǎnfàn	12
evening party	wǎnhuì	11
every	měi	15
everybody	dàjiā	12
exactly!	kě bushì ma!	25
(be) exactly	jiùshi	19
examination	kǎoshì	13
except	chúle..(yǐwài)...dōu	28
exchange	jiāoliú	40
exercise	liànxí	5
expensive	guì	28
explain	jiǎng	12
explain	jiěshi	35
extremely	adj + dehěn	30
extremely	adj + jíle	17
extremely	fēicháng	13

F

face	liǎn	17
factory	gōngchǎng	27
fall (season)	qiūtian	23
fall off	diào	31
family	jiā	14
famous	yǒumíng	14
far	yuǎn	36
fast	kuài	10
father	fùqin	19
feel	gǎndào	36
feel	gǎnjué	24
feel	juéde	17
feel strange	qíguài	20
feel strongly	rènwéi	24
feeling	gǎnjué	24
female	nǚ	23
few	shǎo	2
field of concentration	zhuānyè	35
finally	zuìhòu	33
finish	wán	16
first-rate	dìyīliú	37

G

go out	chū	18
go over	guòqu	23
go to...	dào...qù	8
going to	yào	8
good	hǎo	2
good (be good enough)	xíng	16
good morning	zǎo	30
good-looking	hǎokàn	9
goodbye	zàijiàn	20
graduate	bìyè	38
graduation	bìyè	38
grammar	yǔfǎ	12
grandfather	zǔfù	38
green	lǜ	26
grow (increase)	zēngjiā	24
grow (increase)	zēngzhǎng	40

H

habit	xíguàn	19
hair	tóufa	34
half	bàn	7
hand in	jiāo	14
hang	guà	31
happen (occur)	fāshēng	24
happy	gāoxìng	10
happy	kuàilè	40
Harvard	Hǎfó	11
have	yǒu	2
have fun	wár	11
have no choice but to	zhǐhǎo	37
have not	méiyou	2
have a strong opinion (of)	rènwéi	24
have to	bìxū	15
have to	děi	13
he	tā	1
head	tóu	17
health	shēntǐ	21
hear	tīngjian	16
hear about, hear of	tīngshuō	30
heartily	rèliè	40
heavy	zhòng	31
hello! (answering telephone)	wèi	20
help	bāngmáng	39
help	bāngzhù	31
her	tā	9
here	zhèr (zhèlǐ)	8
high	gāo	16
high school	zhōngxué	35
highway	gōnglù	39

hill	shān	18
him	tā	1
history	lìshǐ	35
history of..	-shǐ	21
hit	dǎ	13
hold (a ceremony)	jǔxíng	38
hold a class	shàngkè	15
hold a meeting	kāihuì	16
home	jiā	14
hope	xīwàng	21
hospital	yīyuàn	20
hot	rè	17
hotel	lǚguǎn	38
hour	xiǎoshí	33
hour	zhōngtóu	25
house	fángzi	28
how	zénme	6
how + adj	duó(me) + adj	36
how about	zěnmeyàng	6
how many	duōshao	4
how many	jǐ	4
hundred	bǎi	27
hungry	è	22
husband	àiren	38
husband	xiānsheng	30

I

I	wǒ	1
idea	zhúyi	31
if	rúguǒ	35
if...then...	yàoshi...jiù...	15
if only...then...	zhǐyào...jiù...	35
illness	bìng	20
important	zhòngyào	14
impression	yìnxiang	40
improve	tígāo	30
improved	jìnbù	30
in a moment	yīhuǐr	20
in addition to	chúle...(yǐwài)...hái	28
in addition to	hái	11
in order to	wèi	34
in the city	chénglǐ	18
increase	zēngjiā	24
increase	zēngzhǎng	40
indefinite number	duō	21
inexpensive	piányi	18
...ing	zhèngzai...ne	23
inside	lǐbian(r)	9
institute	xuéyuàn	34

interest	xìngqu	40
interesting	yǒuyìsi	5
intersection (of streets)	jiēkǒu	36
introduce	jièshào	24
invite	qǐng	16
it	tā	22
it does not matter	méiguānxi	13
it's a pity	kěxī	29

J

Japan	Rìběn	6
Japanese language	Rìyǔ	5
just	gāng	16

K

keep on	lǎo	29
kind	yàngr	37
kind	zhǒng	15
kitchen	chúfáng	40
know	zhīdao	6
know how	huì	5

L

language	yǔyán	34
last year	qùnián	23
late	wǎn	11
laugh	xiào	33
learn	xué	5
learn	xuéxí	4
leave	líkāi	40
leave	zǒu	12
lecture	jiǎnghuà	27
left side	zuǒbian(r)	9
lend	jiè	17
let	ràng	23
letter	xìn	21
level of proficiency	shuǐpíng	16
library	túshūguǎn	9
lie down	tǎng	33
life	shēnghuó	24
light (color)	qiǎn	26
like	xǐhuan	8
likely to	huì	13

liquor	jiǔ	32
listen	tīng	12
literature	wénxué	35
live	zhù	19
lively	huópo	40
long	cháng	3
long time no see	hǎojiǔbùjiàn	39
look at	kàn	4
look for	zhǎo	13
look up	chá	29
lose	diū	27
lots of	xǔduō	30
loudly	dàshēng(r)	29
love	ài	26
low	dī	16
lunch	wǔfàn	33

M

magazine	zázhì	9
make (force)	ràng	23
make	zuò	5
male	nán	23
many	duō	2
many	xǔduō	30
Mary	Mǎlì	34
master	zhǎngwò	14
matter	shìqing	14
may	kěyǐ	13
May Fourth	wǔsì	34
maybe	yěxǔ	16
me	wǒ	1
meaning	yìsi	14
Measure Words		
a cup of	bēi	37
a kind of	zhǒng	15
a package of	bāo	32
a piece (lump, chunk) of	kuài	26
a piece (slice) of	piàn	20
academic course	mén	35
action	cì	22
bed	zhāng	2
bound objects (books, notebooks, etc.)	běn	2
building	zuò	28
business concern	jiā	22
chair	bǎ	5
clothing	jiàn	16

general	ge	2
letter	fēng	40
machine, equipment	tái	32
matter, affair	jiàn	16
mountain	zuò	28
newspaper	zhāng	2
paper	zhāng	2
pen	zhǐ	3
pencil	zhǐ	3
people	ge	2
people (polite)	wèi	6
picture	zhāng	2
record	zhāng	2
room	jiān	18
sentence	jù	12
street	tiáo	36
stroke	bǐ, huà	25
table	zhāng	2
vehicle	liàng	18
writing brush	zhǐ	3
writing utensil	zhǐ	3
medicine	yào	20
meet	yùjian	12
mention	tì	33
method	fāngfǎ	15
middle	zhōngjiàn(r)	9
mile	yīnglǐ	37
minute	fēn	7
Miss	xiǎojiě	24
modern	jìndài	34
money	qián	27
month	yuè	7
(the) more... (the) more...	yuè...yuè...	34
morning	shàngwu	8
morning	zǎoshang	33
(the) most	zuì	25
mother	mǔqin	19
mountain	shān	18
move (something heavy)	bān	18
move residence	bānjiā	26
movie	diànyǐng(r)	8
Mr.	xiānsheng	30
Mrs.	tàitai	30
muddle-headed	hútu	39
music	yīnyuè	29
must	bìxū	15
must	děi	13
mutually	hùxiāng	15

name	míngzi	6
nation	guójiā	30
national anthem	guógē(r)	10
near	jìn	36
need	xūyào	30
never	cónglái (bù/méi)	35
new	xīn	2
New York	Niǔyuē	29
newspaper	bào	1
next	xià	11
night (in the night)	yèli	35
nine	jiǔ	4
no	bù	1
noise	shēngyin	26
not	bù	1
not bad	bùcuò	12
not free (busy)	yǒushèr	8
not only...but also	bùdàn...érqiě	29
not only...but also	yòu...yòu...	28
not until	cái	11
notice	tōngzhī	14
novel	xiǎoshuō(r)	21
now	xiànzài	7
number	hào	39

o'clock	diǎnzhōng	7
occur	fāshēng	24
ocean	hǎi	37
of course	dāngrán	15
oh dear	zāogāo	27
old	jiù	2
old	lǎo	2
one	yī	2
oneself	zìjǐ	10
only	cái	12
only	zhǐ	4
open	kāi	17
opportunity	jīhui	33
or (question)	háishi	5
or (statement)	huòzhě	21
order someone to...	jiào	20
ordinal day of month	hào	7
ordinal prefix	dì	6
organize	zǔzhī	32
originally	běnlái	37

other people	biéren	16
others	biéde	14
otherwise	bùrán	29
outside	wàibian(r)	9
overcoat	dàyī	23
overcome	kèfú	32

P

package	bāo	32
paper	zhǐ	2
parents	fùmǔ	19
park	gōngyuán(r)	36
park (a car)	tíng	27
participate	cānjiā	11
particles		
adverbial	de	13
complement of degree	de	10
potential complement	de	17
completion	le	11
continuation	zhe	23
interjection	ya	39
question	ma	1
question	ne	4
rhetorical	la	39
subordinate (possession)	de	3
suggestion, confirmation	ba	6
parts of (fraction or percent)	fēnzhī	24
pass by	guò	22
pass by	jīngguò	36
pass time	guò	7
past experience suffix	-guo	22
pastry	diǎnxin	26
patient	bìngren	21
pay	fù	28
pay attention to	zhùyì	14
Peking	Běijīng	2
pen	bǐ	3
pencil	qiānbǐ	3
people (of a nation)	rénmín	5
perform, give a performance	biǎoyǎn	29
person	rén	1
photograph	xiàngpiān(r)	31
pick up	ná	15
pictorial	huàbào	5
picture	huàr	25
place	dìfang	9
plan, to plan	jìhua	29
play (ball)	dǎ (qiú)	13
play (drama)	huàjù	14

play (have fun)	wár	11
play (drama)	xì	37
Please may I ask...	qǐngwèn...	36
plural pronoun suffix	-men	3
poetic	yǒushīyì	36
polite	kèqi	19
population	rénkǒu	24
positive (enthusiastic)	jījí	10
post office	yóujú	36
practice	liànxí	5
prepare	zhǔnbèi	13
pretty	piàoliang	23
pretty good	bùcuò	12
previous (month, week, time)	shàng	14
probably	dàgài	36
produce	shēngchǎn	27
produce...effect	qǐ...zuòyong	40
program	jiémù	32
progress	jìnbù	30
pronunciation	fāyīn	31
push	tuī	31
put	fàng	31

Q

quarter (of an hour)	kè	7
question	wèntí	15
question particle	ma	1
question particle	ne	4
quickly	kuàikuārde	13
quiet	ānjìng	26

R

radio	shōuyīnjī	18
rain	xiàyǔ	23
raincoat	yǔyī	33
raise	tígāo	30
reach	dào	19
reach	zháo	16
read	kàn	4
read	kànshū	10
read aloud	niàn	12
real, really	zhēn	23
recent, recently	zuìjìn	30
recognize	rènshi	12
record (gramophone)	chàngpiān(r)	34
record (write down)	jì	25

red	hóng	17
remember	jì	25
remember	jìde	33
rent	fángqian	28
repair	xiūlǐ	32
report	bàogào	14
represent	dàibiǎo	38
research (do research in)	yánjiū	34
resemble	xiàng	22
reserve	dìng	38
respect (aspect)	fāngmiàn	35
rest	xiūxi	14
restaurant	fànguǎn(r)	22
result	jiéguǒ	38
return (things borrowed)	huán	21
return (come/go back)	huí...(lai/qu)	18
review	fùxí	12
right!	duìle	3
right away	lìkè	24
right side	yòubian(r)	9
rise	qǐ	28
road	lù	36
room	fángjiān	38
room	wūzi	18
room for...	-shǐ	34
roommate	tóngwū	6
route	lù	36
run	pǎo	31
run a temperature	fāshāo	20
running water	zìláishuǐ	27

S

satisfied	mǎnyì	37
school	xuéxiào	5
school term	xuéqī	11
schoolmate	tóngxué	14
schoolyard	xiàoyuán(r)	36
sea	hǎi	37
seat	zuòwei	37
see	kànjian	16
see each other	jiànmiàn	39
seek out	zhǎo	13
seems (it seems to be)	hǎoxiàng	23
self-study	zìxué	9
sell	mài	15
sentence	jùzi	12
settled	dìng	39
seven	qī	4
Shanghai	Shànghǎi	38
shape	yàngzi	26

she	tā	11
ship building	zàochuán	38
shirt	chènshān	37
short	duǎn	3
should	yīnggāi	13
sick, to be sick	bìng	20
side	pángbiān(r)	9
simple	jiǎndān	25
simplified	jiǎnhuà	25
simplified style	jiǎntǐ	25
simply!	jiǎnzhí	32
simultaneously	tóngshí	24
since	cóng...qǐ	24
sing	chànggē(r)	10
sit	zuò	17
sit astride	qí	18
six	liù	4
skillful in	huì	5
sleep	shuì	28
sleep	shuìjiào	29
slow	màn	10
slowly	mànmārde	13
small	xiǎo	2
smile	xiào	33
smoke	xīyān	32
snow	xiàxuě	23
so long as	zhǐyào...jiù	35
solve	jiějué	30
some	jǐ	17
some	yīxiē	5
some	yǒude	15
some people	yǒurén	25
sometimes	yǒushíhou(r)	9
somewhat	yǒu(yi)diǎr	17
sorry, I am sorry	duìbuqǐ	20
sorry, I am sorry	duìbuzhù	35
sound	shēngyin	26
south, southern	nánfāng	22
speak	shuōhuà	10
special	tèbié	10
spring	chūntian	23
spring festival	chūnjié	22
spring vacation	chūnjià	29
stand	zhàn	17
station	zhàn	36
stay	zhù	19
still	hái	13
story	gùshi	34
strange	qíguài	20
street	jiē	24
strike (hit)	dǎ	20
strokes (of a pen)	bǐhuà	25

student	xuésheng	1
study	niànshū	10
study	xué	5
study	xuéxí	4
study abroad	liúxué	40
style	yàngzi	26
style	yàngr	37
succeed in	chéng, dào, zháo	17
sugar	táng	31
suitable	héshì	28
summer	xiàtian	23
supper	wǎnfàn	12
sweater	máoyī	26
swim	yóuyǒng	37

T

table	zhuōzi	5
Taipei	Táiběi	19
take	ná	15
take a lot (money, time)	fèi	18
take a walk	sànbù	24
take pictures	zhàoxiàng	38
take to (a place)	sòng	21
take with	dài	18
talk	shuōhuà	10
talk	tánhuà	19
tall	gāo	40
tall building	dàlóu	28
tea	chá	32
teach	jiāo	4
teach	jiāoshū	10
teacher	jiàoshī	19
teacher	lǎoshī	1
telephone	diànhuà	20
television (set)	diànshì(jī)	32
tell	gàosu	15
ten	shí	4
ten thousand	wàn	38
tense	jǐnzhāng	32
test	kǎoshì	13
text	kèwén	12
textbook	kèběn	16
than	bǐ	23
thank you	xièxie	4
that	nà, nèi	1
that much	nènme	11
that way	nènme	11
then	jiù	12
there	nàr	8

thesis	lùnwén	29
thing	dōngxi	11
think	xiǎng	13
think (have a strong opinion)	rènwéi	24
think wrongly	yǐwéi	37
this	zhè, zhèi	1
this much	zènme	11
this way	zènme	11
this year	jīnnián	7
thought	sīxiǎng	34
thousand	qiān	35
three	sān	2
ticket	piào(zi)	38
time	shíhou(r)	7
time	shíjiān	18
time difference	shíchā	40
tired	lèi	37
to	dào	8
to	duì	21, 32
to	duìyú	40
to	gěi	21
today	jīntiān	7
together	yīkuàr	33
together	yīqǐ	8
toilet	cèsuǒ	26
Tokyo	Dōngjīng	39
tomorrow	míngtiān	12
too (also)	yě	4
too + adj	tài + adj (le)	10
too bad	kěxī	29
top	shàngbian(r)	9
topic	tímù	34
towards	duì	21, 32
towards	duìyú	40
towards	wàng	36
traditional style	fántǐ	25
train	huǒchē	36
translate	fānyì	21
travel	lǚxíng	29
try	shì	17
try to recognize	rèn	25
turn	zhuǎn	36
turn off	guān(shang)	28
two	èr	4
two	liǎng	2

U

ugly	nánkàn	31
unceasingly	bùduànde	40

unceasingly	bùtíngde	14
understand	dǒng	6
university	dàxué	6
unneeded	yòngbuzháo	31
unusual	tèbié	10
USA	Měiguó	1
use	yòng	5
used (old)	jiù	2
(be) used to	xíguàn	19
useful	yǒuyòng	15

V

vacation, have vacation	fàngjià	22
various	gè	33
various places	gèchù	37
very	fēicháng	13
very	hěn	2
vicinity	fùjìn	28
visit (a place)	cānguān	37
vocabulary	shēngcí	12

W

wait	děng	39
wait until	děng...zai	38
wake up	xǐng	40
walk	zǒu	12
walk	zǒulù	20
wall	qiáng	3
want to	xiǎng	13
want to	yào	8
warm	nuǎnhuo	23
warm (compassionate)	rèqíng	21
wash	xǐ	27
Washington	Huáshèngdùn	37
watch	biǎo	26
way (method)	fāngfǎ	15
way (to deal with difficulty)	bànfa	13
wear	chuān	23
weather	tiānqì	23
week	xīngqī	7
weekend	zhōumò	37
welcome	huānyíng	18
west, western	xīfāng	35
what	shénme	6
What is there to do?	zěnmebàn	15
where	nǎr	8

which	něi	6
white	bái	26
who	shéi	6
why	wèishénme	8
wife	àiren	38
wife	tàitai	30
will (is going to)	yào	8
will do (good enough)	xíng	16
window	chuānghu	17
wine	jiǔ	32
winter	dōngtian	23
wish you	zhù	21
with	gēn	8
work	gōngzuò	4
write	xiězì	10
writing brush	máobǐ	3
wrong	cuò	22

Y

Yamamoto	Shānběn (Japanese surname)	6
year	nián	7
year at school	niánjí	11
yellow	huáng	26
yesterday	zuótiān	11
yet	hái	11
you	nǐ	1
you (polite)	nín	1
young	niánqīng	34
younger brother	dìdi	19
younger sister	mèimei	19
youth	qīngnián	40

Z

zero	líng	7